Stones of Glory
Historical Timeline

Richard Fellows

Copyright © 2024 by Richard Fellows

STONES OF GLORY

All rights reserved.

First Published 2024

Richard Fellows reserves the moral right to be identified as the author of this work. Short extracts and brief quotations may be copied for non-profit personal use only, without prior permission. Otherwise, no part of this publication may be reproduced, stored in a retrieval system, or transmitted in any form or by any means, electronic, mechanical, photocopying, scanning or otherwise, without the prior written consent of the author.

Cover Image: 289783110 © Zuberka | Dreamstime.com
Cover Design: Bettina Kradolfer

Most Scripture references are from the New King James Version. Copyright © 1982 by Thomas Nelson, Inc. Used by permission. All rights reserved.

Scripture quotations marked (NIV), taken from The Holy Bible, New International Version® (NIV®) Copyright© 1973, 1978, 1984, 2011 by Biblica, Inc.® Used by permission.www.biblica.com.

Printed Soft-cover edition: 978-0-6485883-9-9

"She came to Jerusalem with a very great retinue,
with camels that bore spices, very much gold,
and precious stones to help Solomon."
(1 Kings 10:2)[1]

---

[1] The Queen of Sheba came by God's providence to help King Solomon. Many of us will experience camel moments where divine help comes at the perfect time through people.

DEDICATION

Steve & Hayley Fahey

&

Jason Cobb

Thank you, Steve and Hayley Fahey for your strong friendship and abundant love over the many years.

Thank you, Jason Cobb, for being a Rock in my life. Both beautiful families have enriched my life with great strength and support. I honour you both, and without your love and generosity this book would not be in existence.

FOREWORD

Stones of Glory is one of the world's most comprehensive investigations and modern theological explorations into the manifestation of heaven stones on Earth.

Having witnessed first-hand the extraordinary phenomenon of heaven stones materializing on Earth, I have also observed the profound impact it has on those who witness this miraculous event unfold. Reactions vary from cautiousness and offence to perplexity and consideration of monetary value. Others are captivated by a sense of awe, wonder, and devotion to God's tangible presence.

Out of the hundreds who have witnessed this unique manifestation, only one person, Richard Fellows, has been profoundly impacted to the extent of dedicating a decade-long pursuit to uncovering the truth behind it. This book is a testament to his passionate quest to illuminate biblical history, Jewish traditions, and modern-day encounters with heaven stones.

As the union of Heaven and Earth intensifies through Christ Jesus (Ephesians 1:10), this book will serve as the essential guide to help individuals grasp the divine purpose unfolding on Earth.

May this book enrich your faith and increase your sense of childlike wonder as you become His glorious living stone.

Jason Cobb - *The Life Foundation, New Zealand, 2024*

INTRODUCTION:
Stones of Glory

Stones of Glory was birthed out of a never-ending passion to understand the stones of heaven. God said in his Word that the stones would cry out if we were to stay silent (Luke 19:40-44), and they have been crying out throughout history with their appearance in different forms. The heaven stones appear in times of closeness to God and high praise, but they also appear in seasons to quicken dull hearts to His reality. For God has left a witness throughout history of the workings of His spiritual Kingdom[2]. Their main outflow into the earth is due to heavenly intimacy to give revelation and spiritual significance in the work of joining (merging) heaven into the earth as one realm fully open. The stones are a token and record of glory.

In 2019, I wrote my first book called *Wilderness Like Eden*, which was brought into the world from my experiences of staying with a group of friends in an Orphanage in India in the remote mountains. In that book, I documented and provided research from testimonies and the Bible, including Jewish Theology and commentaries and Rabbinical traditions on the supernatural manifestation of gemstones from heaven. I went on a fascinating journey of study, revealing that this occurrence wasn't some scam. *Wilderness Like Eden* - gave a basic Theology

---

[2] "God, who at various times and in various ways spoke in time past to the fathers by the prophets" (Hebrew 1:1) - "Yet *He did* not *leave* Himself without a *witness—He did* good by giving you rain from heaven and fruitful seasons, filling your hearts with joy and gladness." (Acts 14:17) - "For since the creation of the world His invisible attributes are clearly seen, being understood by things that are made " (Romans 1:20) - even heaven stones.

and testimonies of the stones, but it was not a full historical account. I have to admit it was the best research we had at our finger tips in the beginning. It was a very useful start (resource) as many were grasping in the dark to comprehend this phenomenon[3].

This phenomenon has not died out and there are still currant reports of heaven stones manifesting today[4]. After writing my first book, *Wilderness Like Eden*, my heart was still deeply driven to search for more research. I would spend hours searching the internet and hard to find books for references. As the years passed by, I would come across new accounts, new research and new revelation diligently recording them in a notebook. There have been many days of reflection.

I can remember a friend sharing a heaven encounter they had where they visited a place in the Father's garden called in their terms, "the pool of tears" (Ocean of Tears)[5]. This revelation really moved my heart to tears, it was so beautiful that I was determined to see if any other Seer's throughout history had seen this place. After months of searching, I found some Jewish texts that spoke about this place called the "Ocean of Tears" in the Father's garden. I was stunned with amazement. Then I came across a number of early Christian Mystics who had brought down physical jewellery from heaven. This again stirred the flame of my heart.

---

[3] It was not the best because I had written it, but because of what I had been able to research and gather together at the time.
[4] Senior Pastor Othusite Mmusi and founder at Glory Invasion International Church has witnessed many gemstones manifest this year - 2024.
[5] Her account is beautifully recalled in the book, "Talk With Me In Paradise", by Angela Curtis.

As I came upon more and more new research, I decided to do a Podcast called, "Stones of Glory," a historical timeline where I started to put together a timeline from eternity to the present day of gemstone appearances from above. I thought I had exhausted the research, but I kept coming across more accounts and more significant dates.

Due to being a systematic Theologian who grasps to document every detail, line by line, step by step - my heart started to be quickened and moved to write this book "Stones of Glory." To document every line of evidence and connect the fine details writing a systematic historical account of the gemstone phenomenon with as many dates as possible.

In the early days when I and others encountered the stones manifesting there was a lot of scepticism, many people didn't believe the stones were from God or that God was interested in giving stones. I think this book will show that God has never stopped manifesting His stones from the days of Adam and Eve to the present. The person who doubts the phenomenon is one who has never really read religious texts or studied history carefully!

I think you will see by just reading the Contents pages – that it gives a comprehensive analytical outline that the evidence is considerable and in-depth and almost exhaustive.

I can remember when I was in Bible College and it was our last few days before we graduated. During our send-off gathering, I was prayed over by a Prophet. He said to me, that "God would use my life to polish me and continue to polish different subjects to give an exact answer" - this I believe is part of the fulfilment in print.

This book is about the supernatural gemstones from heaven and their materialization in physical form in the earth. Heaven is full of gemstones as this book will reveal but they have a spiritual purpose and use behind them. Throughout history there has been many seasons from generation to generation where supernatural gemstones have appeared from heaven through the spiritual veil. Like God chose Adam and Eve first, and then Israel, of which the chosen nation was to be a tutor to the nations of the world (gentiles in Christ), the gemstones have appeared at different times to all. What some have heard and witnessed that supernatural gemstones are appearing in Christian meetings in atmospheres of high praise and worship in recent years is not some new fad or deception scam. Its roots and timelines can be traced all through history. This book takes up the challenge to document this occurrence with great detail and insights of divine revelation, evidence, ancient texts, dates and testimonies to produce a clear timeline record.

I am sure there are many names (people who have received stones) that could be added to the timeline, who have experienced this phenomenon. I present my 13 years of research on the subject and there may be some names missing as one would expect, but I believe I have enough that place "close enough dates" together to reveal generational seasons. There is a consistent flow of dates documented revealing the phenomenon in history.

At this stage before we dive into the depths of research it will be good if I give some simple *definitions* and *explanations* on where these stones come from and how they come to earth. I will keep it very brief as the process will be explained later in great theological detail.

* The stones come out of God the creator of all things. (Colossians 1:14)
* Heaven is full of gemstones. (Revelation 21:12)
* The river of God from the throne pours out and stones flow out of God and 'arc' off into the crystal sea. (Revelation 4:6)
* They come down through the spiritual veil from God. (Hebrews 6:19)
* They come down from the rivers of Eden through portals into the earth. (Genesis 28:10-19)
* Angels bring them down. (Hebrews 1:14)
* In atmospheres of high praise and worship they "form" through the veil. (Hebrews 11:1)
* People in visions or heaven encounters/trances receive them in heaven, and on leaving their encounter they open their eyes on earth and in their hand is the stone. (Ezekiel 1:1)

Scripture support

Behind the physical world, is the spiritual veil - *"Enters the presence behind the veil" (Hebrews 6:19)*

Rich atmosphere portals open - *"This is the house of God, and the gate of heaven" (Genesis 28:10-19) - "He saw a stairway resting on the earth, with its top reaching the heavens. He saw the angels of God ascending and descending on it."*

Angels minister and bring spiritual goods - *"Are they not all ministering spirits sent forth to minister for those who will inherit salvation." (Hebrews 1:14)*

Eyes and portals open - *"Heavens were opened, and I saw visions of God (Ezekiel 1:1)*

Our spiritual bodies are caught up, while our earthly bodies are on earth - *"In the same way there are earthly bodies and heavenly bodies. There is a splendour of the celestial body, and a different one for the earthy." (1 Corinthians 15:40)*

Caught up - *"Was caught up to the third heaven in paradise, whether in the body or out of the body, I do not know." (2 Corinthians 11:2-3)*

Ascending into heaven - *"I looked, and behold a door standing open in heaven. And the first voice... speaking with me, saying, 'Come up here, and I will show you things which must take place after this.' Immediately I was in the Spirit, and behold set in heaven and sat on a throne." (Revelation 4:1)*

Spiritual faith manifests the stones - *"Now faith is the substance of things hoped for, the evidence of things not seen." (Hebrews 11:1)* - Faith brings what is in the spiritual realm (heaven), that is not seen in the earth to manifest in the earth as substance.

Divine Revelation and Spiritual Significance of the Stones

* A token of remembrance of God's creative works - The crystal sea holds the record of God's creative works and the stones flow out as tokens (Revelation 4:6)
* They hold a record of our spiritual works - "If any one's work (gold, silver, precious stones), which he has built on endures, he will receive a reward" (1 Corinthians 2:14)
* The stones can come with angels for ministry - "Are they not all ministering spirits sent forth to minister for those who will inherit salvation." (Hebrews 1:14)

* Be given as gifts for the Bride - "He has given us every spiritual blessing from heavenly places in Christ." (Ephesian 1:3) - "Every good gift and perfect gift is from above, and comes down from the Father." (James 1:17)
* The Bride is adorned with function stones - "As a bride adorns herself with her jewels." (Isaiah 61:10)
* The stones can hold Kingdom presence and power - "To him who overcomes I will give some of the manna to eat. And I will give them a white stone." (Revelation 2:17)
* The stones can shift the healing of creation by their frequency of God's power - "Spiritual blessings/ healing" (Ephesian 1:3) - If God can put power into wood to heal water, He can put power into stones to heal creation behind the veil - "When they came to Marah, they could not drink its water because it was bitter. Then Moses cried out to the Lord, and the Lord showed him a piece of wood. He threw it into the water, and the water became fit to drink." (Exodus 15:22).[6]
* Also stones flow into the crystal sea[7], but also healing leaves flow from that river down into the earth behind the veil to heal creation (stones and healing leaves) - Ezekiel's heavenly temple shows that where ever the river goes it brings life to creation. The stones, the leaves, flow from the water of the sanctuary (out of Eden from the throne), and their fruit will be for food and their leaves and stones for healing." (Ezekiel 47:7- 40-48 - Revelation 21)
* The stones are a witness - "the stones would cry out if we were to stay silent" (Luke 19:40-44)

---

[6] Gods healing anointing power can also reside in a dead man's bones, "When the body touched Elisha's bones, the man came to life and stood up on his feet." (2 Kings 13:20), and also in handkerchiefs and aprons." (Acts 19:11-12)

[7] A river flows down from the crystal sea into Eden to water the garden (earth) and the stones are in it (Genesis 2:10)

* God's goal was to finish his plan when the right time came. He planned that all things in heaven and on earth be joined together with Christ as the head" (Ephesian 1:10) - and renew creation "As the new heavens and the new earth that I make will endure before me." (Isaiah 66:22)
* And more...

Now that we have set a basic understanding of the stones we will journey on to the realms of heaven with Father God on His throne. The Father's body inlaid with sapphires and our hidden existence. Let the stones shine their GLORY!

This is my *"Magnum Opus"* on the heavenly stones.

ANALYTICAL OUTLINE

The * Symbol lists "some" of the topics covered under the Headings.

Father God's body Inlaid with Sapphires ...……………………………......21
* The Skin of God.
* For in Him we live and move and exist.
* God sits on a sapphire throne.

The Crystal Sea; Full of Precious Stones …………………………………… 24
* We are the Temple of precious stones come forth out of the womb of the dawn.
* The Stones of Fire.

Physical Precious Stones - God's Creative Works …………………………….. 27
* Cave to the Fathers Garden under the Throne.
* Pearls - Children of light.
* Reb Yitzchak Vorker.
* The Ocean of Tears.
* Your righteousness is like the mighty mountain, your justice like the great Ocean.
* Bottles of Tears and the Wall of Remembrance.
* Tears of intercession and the heavenly wailing Wall.
* You keep track of my wanderings and my weeping. You have stored my many tears in your bottle - not one will be lost.
* Tears of Warfare.
* Angels take our bottled tears and pour them on their weapons to fight for our deliverances.
* Jan's encounter - Ocean of Tears.
* Greek and Jewish stories of Tears turning into precious stones.
* The Testament of Abraham; Tears turn into precious stones.
* Islamic Story; Adam & Eve's Tears turned into precious stones.
* The legend of Sinbad's journey in Ceylon
* Recent tears turning into precious stones.
* Two types of categories for the stones 1, Our existence and 2, Spiritual

physical tokens of God's creative works.

The Four Rivers of the Crystal Sea 40

* The Pishon River, there is gold and precious stones.
* They came down from the Throne to earth through the spiritual river/realm.
* Physical stones in the river/spirit - And we came down as precious stones in the spirit.
* Adam the first King and Priest.
* Adam's precious stone book.

The Wilderness 42

* Moses's Sapphire Tablets.
* The Urim and Thummim Stones.
* Precious stones and pearls rained down from heaven along with the manna in the wilderness.
* The Testament of Solomon, describes the angel Michael giving Solomon a powerful ring from heaven, with an engraved precious stone.

Jesus Adorns the Bride, 33 AD 48

* Bride adorns herself with her jewels.
* Temple Bride.

Apostle John - Book of Revelation – 95 AD 51

* And I will give him a white stone.

Early Church Fathers Interpretations 52

* Hippolytus of Rome, (early 3rd century).
* Victorinus of Pettau, (late 3rd century).
* Caesarius of Arles (late 5th to early 6th century) and the Venerable Bede (late 6th to early 7th century).
* Andrew of Caesarea (late 6th to early 7th century).

Meaning and Purposes, Sizes and Colours 54

* What the stones carry and mean.

Gold and Money Appears! 56

* St. Benedict (543 AD) - Gold
* St. Dominic (1170 AD) - Money.

* St. Lydwine (1433 AD) - Purse never runs out.
* Jan Rainbow - Pocket never runs out.
* ATM's, Bank Accounts and Money.
* My Experience.

Mystical Jewellery! The Mystics! 60

* Lucy of Narni, early (1500s AD)
* Stephana Quinzani, (1457 AD)
* St. Colette (1447 AD)
* St. Catherine dei Ricci (1542 AD)
* St. Veronica Giulinai (1727 AD)
* St. Jean Marie (1859 AD)
* Golden Candlestick Ladies 1948 AD
* Children in India (2009)

The Prophecy of the Stones in the 1980s 66

* Glenn Smith received back in the 1980s,

Ruth Ward Heflin 68

* Gold Dust and Jewels.

Gold Dust and Gold Teeth 69

* Gold fillings 1800s AD.
* Gold Dust and Dental work - 1960-1980 AD.
* Gold Dust, Silver Dust, Sapphire Dust, Gold Nuggets - 1998 AD.
* Gold Teeth.
* Siteri Saurara – Rainbow Dust on Pillow.

Stones Start Appearing all around the World 72

* 2000 AD
* 2004 AD
* 2006 AD
* 2007 AD
* 2008 AD
* 2012 AD

MY First Exposure! 79

* My Encounters in India.

- * Jason Cobb, Orphanage India 2009 AD.
- * Other People Encountering Stones.

Stones Manifest Throughout NZ 85
- * 2014 AD
- * 2015 AD
- * 2019 AD
- * 2023 AD

Important Historical Dates 88
- * 1446 – 2024 AD

Intermediate Realm 90
- * Near Death Experience.
- * Stones the Blue-print of your life.
- * Record of life in Stone.

In Heaven – Crossed Over! 94
- * Those in heaven can send stones down.

Looking around Heaven (Stones) 95
- * Enoch.
- * Ian Clayton.
- * Jan Rainbow.
- * Seneca Sodi's Visitation to Paradise.
- * Oden Hetrick.
- * A Child's Testimony.

Atmosphere of Praise! Loss and Gains 101
- * Praise, Worship, Residue and the Veil.

Treasure Rooms and lost Property 102
- * Buildings and walls that hold our treasure.
- * People have secured for themselves, as well as rejected blessings.
- * Seneca Sodi's experience.
- * Jan Rainbows experience.

Jesus the Master Carpenter/Jeweller 104

* Crown of Life.
* Victor's Crown.
* Heaven Encounter.

The Apostles Foundation Stones 107

City of God Revealed 108

The Seven Mountains 110

* Enoch and the Seven Mountains of precious stones.

Wheels of Beryl 113

* Angelic, Chariots, Gemstones.

Christianity and Gems 115

* History of Gemstones in the early Church.

Birth Stones and the Bible 119

* History of Birth Stones.
* 12 Tribes, 12 Stones and 12 Zodiac Signs.
* Jewish Historian Josephus - His Interpretation.
* Church Fathers - Interpretations.
* We will be as the multitude of the stars - Set in the sky to mark seasons, days and years.
* Heaven Testimony.

Church Fathers and the healing benefits of Gemstones 124

* Saint Basil the Great (4th century AD)
* Saint Isidore of Seville (7th century AD)
* Christian clergy - 12th to 14th centuries - "lithotherapy"
* Dominican monk Albertus Magnus (c. 1193-1280)
* Early Medieval writers

The Kingdom is the Present Future 126

* Foretastes, foreshadowing the powers of the age to come.

Precious Stones in Blood 128

- Saint Philomena

Stones as Beacons of Frequency **129**

Jesus was Well Aware of Heaven Stones **131**
- Stone Terminology.

Attitudes of the Heart **135**

Objections from Critics... **139**
- Gemologists documentation.

Don't cast Your pearls **146**

Church Fathers; Rock of the Soul.. **148**

The Scriptures... **153**

Bibliography **170**

Father God's Body Inlaid with Sapphires

The Father's body is encased within a garment of light shining forth His eternal glory.

> *"You are clothed with glory and majesty,*
> *Who covers Yourself with light as with a garment."*
> *(Psalm 104:1-2)*

The Father of creation is a being with arms and legs[8] and behind the veil of His light, His body is covered with gemstones. The stones are a part of His skin and reflect His nature and image. The Father we are told walked in the garden as a spirit being (Genesis 3:8). Many have interpreted the book of Song of Solomon as being a love relationship between God the groom and the woman as His bride (the saints).[9]

If this is the case then on a deeper spiritual meaning of the text the book of Song of Solomon 5:14-16 is revealing God's true nature,

---

[8] The Ancient of Days was seated, His garment was white as snow, and His hair like pure wool (Daniel 7:9)

[9] The Book of Song of Solomon has been interpreted in the following ways, 1) A love story between Solomon and the Shulamite woman. 2)A love story between Christ and His Church - the mystery of marriage is to show Christ's love for His Church. 3)God's love towards a believer's soul. 4)A picture of God and the immaculate conception through Mary. 5)The Kabbalistic Shiur Qomah, describing the groom's body as God's own form or face. 6)The Zohar, describing a dialogue between the feminine and masculine aspects of divinity. 7)Early Syriac Churches believed that God was the groom. 8)God's love for Creation and His People in a betrothal Covenant.

> "His hands are rods of gold set with beryl. His body as bright ivory inlaid with sapphires. His legs are pillars of marble set on bases of fine gold, His countenance is like Lebanon, excellent as the cedars. His mouth is most lovely. This is my beloved, and this is my friend O daughters of Jerusalem." (Song of Solomon 3:14-16)

Yes, the text is not 100% literal, its capturing insights and spiritual truths. But we can grasp, His body is beautifully white with light, and His blue spirit veins appearing under the skin encase the sapphire stones. The stones start in Him... "physical stones and spiritual stones" (spirits) - **"For in Him we live and move** and exist [that is, in Him we actually have our being], as even some of your own poets have said" (Acts 17:23).

Ian Clayton in one of his heaven encounters describes seeing God the Father,

"Let me tell you what God's skin is like - if you could get a mat of diamonds of about five or six carats each, weave them all together like skin, put the colours of the rainbow in it, make it go blue-white, burning and rippling fire and flickering with light, then you have an idea of what His skin is like."[10]

God the Father sits on a sapphire throne[11] and at the edge of the throne a river flows down from it, stones, precious stones "arc" off it falling off and flow down into the river. The river is the Spirit of God, the breath of God, His creative power flowing into all dimensions of creation. These stones are representing an

---

[10] Ian Clayton, Realms of the Kingdom - Volume 1, Seraph Creative Publishers, 2014, p.140

[11] And above the expanse over their heads there was the likeness of a throne, in appearance like sapphire; and seated above the likeness of a throne was a likeness with a human appearance. (Ezekiel 1:26)

aspect of God's image and His creative works, and also our individual existence. They are like tokens capturing precious images and moments in time remembered in a formed stone.

Scripture speaks of two types of stones,

1. We are called precious stones[12], and

2. Precious stones speak of God's creative works,[13] victories, deliverances, protection, and encase spiritual values (gradings, testings, evaluations, mantles, and often as gifts for the bride).[14]

---

[12] "You also, are living stones" (1 Peter 2:5)

[13] The stones also show forth the beauty dimensions of God. The beauty realm!

[14] "O you afflicted one, tossed with tempest an not comforted, behold I will lay your stones with colourful gems, And lay your foundations with sapphires. I will make your pinnacles of rubies, your gates of crystal, and your walls of precious stones." (Isaiah 54:54;11-12) - "If anyone builds on this foundation using gold, silver, precious stones, wood, hay, or straw, his workmanship will be evident, because the Day will bring it to light. It will be revealed with fire, and the fire will prove the quality of each man's work. If what he has built survives, he will receive a reward." (1 Corinthians 3:13)

The Crystal Sea is Full of Precious Stones

> *"Then the angel showed me the river of the water of life, bright as crystal, flowing from the throne of God and of the Lamb through the middle of the street of the city; also, on either side of the river, the tree of life with its twelve kinds of fruit, yielding its fruit each month." (Revelation 22:1)*

> *"I saw before me what seemed to be a **glass sea** mixed with fire. And on it **stood** all the **people** who had been victorious over the beast" (Revelation 15:2)*

Revelation 15:2, is describing the end of history when all believers will stand on the sea of glass victorious over the beast. But it also hints to the beginning of time when precious stones were birthed into the sea (to flow down the river) to start their journey. We came out of Him - to one day in the future stand before Him in awe.

Scripture tells us in Revelation 21:22, that "The Lord is the Temple," and out of Him came created spirits (our existence, from the Father of spirits - Hebrews 12:9). We came out of God and lived under the throne in the place called the treasury of souls. We are called precious stones in Scripture because we came from the true Rock. Moses wrote,

> *"He is the Rock, his works are perfect, and all his ways are just, a faithful God who does no wrong, upright and just is he" (Deuteronomy 32:4)*

> *"Listen to Me, you who follow after righteousness. You who seek the Lord; Look to the Rock from which you were hewn." (Isaiah 51:1).*

We are the spiritual building that completes the Lord's Temple. We were the hidden mystery before the ages, chosen in Him before the foundation of the world dwelling in the secret place under the shadow of the almighty's throne.

> *"You also, as living stones, are being built up a spiritual house, a holy priesthood, to offer up spiritual sacrifices acceptable to God through Jesus Christ." (1 Peter 2:5)*[15]

We came forth out of the womb of the dawn (God) in the beauty of holiness the youth of God's dew[16]. In Zohar 3:128, Idra Rabbah says, this dew is described as "the light of the pale glow of the ancient One." And from that dew exists the supernatural saints." Meaning - We came forth out of God in eternity (our spirits) as a pale glow from the light of God, ours reflecting dimmer than His eternal light, but a copy of His image. Our existence comes from the source of God, that is why when God is called the Rock, we can be called precious stones from God and also dew that glows from coming forth from the His eternal nature as the light of the world - 'In Him was DNA, and the DNA was the light of men" (John 1:4)[17].

Even Lucifer is said to have covered us guarding us as precious stones in the holy fire of God on the Mountain Rock. Speaking of Lucifer, it says, *"You were in Eden, the garden of God - You walked back and forth in the midst of the stones of*

---

[15] We are precious stones in Him, chosen and formed in Him from the foundation of the world, but once we are sent down into the earth we are being built up, polished up to be the true perfected Temple.

[16] Psalm 110:3

[17] In Him we reflect His image as we reflect His DNA.

fire." (Ezekiel 28:13-14). The stones of fire are us forming the Temple of holy fire. Each stone is a soul's DNA[18].

Dinah Dye says, "Eden, the garden sanctuary [19] was the original undefiled bride."[20] - That is "We" as precious stones (symbolic), are part of the Temple, the body of God the bride.

---

[18] Around the "stones of fire" exists thrones the "seats of the gods" - This is the place in Ezekiel 28:2 where the divine council is set up.

[19] A garden sanctuary was a temple.

[20] Dinah Dye, The Temple Revealed In Creation, Foundations of Torah Publishing, 2016, p. 181

Physical Precious Stones - God's Creative Works.

Before the throne the crystal river flows out of God and into a huge crystal sea, which flows around the throne. The river also flows down the streets of the eternal city. At the top of the Mountain of the Lord this sea divides and flows down the Mountain like four streams into rivers, on its way flowing under the throne.

Under the throne half way down the Mountain is a cave. As you go through the cave and out of a forest one comes to the Father's garden, of which many oceans and beaches exist. Heaven encounters have revealed that on these beaches around the Fathers Garden, young children[21] who have never been loved by their parents or died at birth or in their early years are gathered here to be brought up and are visited by the Father and embraced in his arms of love[22]. But one of the many paths in this garden

---

[21] It is interesting that "Pearls" are formed in salt water or among coral reefs. Leslie Harding says, "The Greek name for pearl is morganites, which is the form of the ancient Sanskrit Maracata that was taken at the time it was adopted by the Greeks. The Persian name is Merwerid, which is the nearest to the most ancient form Murwari interpreted as "Pearl" or "a child of light".

[22] This revelation is unpacked more in my book, "The Fathers Garden", and also in the book, "Explore With Me In Paradise" by Angela Curtis. Scripture hints of this place, as below, so above, "So, the seashore will be pastures, with caves for shepherds and folds for flocks. And the coast will be for the remnant of the house of Judah. They will pasture on it. In the house of Ashkelon, they will lie down at evening, for the Lord their God will care for them and restore their fortunes." (Zephaniah 2:6-7)

leads down to a pool, a kind of ocean that is called the Ocean of Tears.

A 2nd century Rabbi, Yitzchak Vorker, spoke of going to Eden to look for a friend. He describes coming to a forest and then to a sea at the end of it. The forest entrance is a little down the Mountain of the Lord and is like a cave that leads under the throne to the Father's Garden. Out from the forest, one walks through the Father's Garden down to an Ocean, some call it a lake, but the Jews called it the "Ocean of Tears". This is where our tears are collected and stored (I cover this in great detail in my book, *Heaven through the Eyes of Children*).

> "Before Reb Yitzchak Vorker left this world, he promised his son that he would contact him from heaven and tell him how things were for him in Gan Eden. But four weeks passed, and his son didn't hear from him. He couldn't understand what was going on, so he went to his father's best friend, Reb Menachem Mendel of Kotsk, and said: "Rebbe, I'm so worried about my holy father. He promised to come back and speak to me, if only in a dream. But it's been four weeks, and I haven't heard anything from him. Do you think something could have happened to him in Heaven?"
> And the Kotzker answered. "The truth is that your father also promised me to come back and tell me what happened to him in the World Above. And I got worried when I didn't hear from him. So, I went up to Heaven to look for him.
> "Let me tell you what happened: I went everywhere in Heaven searching for your father. I went to the palaces of all the tzaddikim, all the holy people – of Rashi, the Rambam, Rabbi Akiva. I visited the place of the prophets, and even went to the very highest levels– to Moshe Rabbeinu and our holy fathers, Abraham, Isaac and Jacob. Everywhere I went, I said, 'I'm looking for my friend, the exalted Reb Yitzchak Vorker. Have you seen him?' And they all told me, 'Yes, he was here. But he didn't stay. He went on....'

I didn't know what to do, where else to go. So finally, I asked the angels, 'Have you seen the holy Reb Yitzchak Vorker? Do you know where he went?' And this time I got an answer, the angels told me, 'If you keep going in this direction, you'll come to a thick dark forest. You must pass through it, and when the forest ends at a sea, that's where you'll find him.'

So, I kept walking through Heaven, and as the angels had said, I soon came to the darkest, most forbidding forest I had ever seen in my life. I wanted to run away. I started to hear a strange sound.

Finally, I came out of the trees, and found myself on the shore of the sea, an ocean so big I couldn't see the other side. And I realized that the sound I'd been hearing was coming from the waves. But it was not the sound that waves usually make... it was more like a wail, a moan, a scream – full of the most desperate pain. Never in my life had I heard waves crying and begging like this... And there at the edge of the ocean, I saw your father, the holy Vorker. He was leaning on his staff, staring at the sea. He never took his eyes off the water. I ran toward him, 'Reb Yitzchak, my holy friend, what is this place? What are you doing here?' He turned towards me, 'Ah Mendel, don't you recognize this ocean?'

'No, what is it? What's that sound? What's going on here?'

'Mendel, let me tell you...this is the Ocean of Tears, the sea of Jewish tears. I want you to know that every tear is so precious to the Master of the World. God takes all the tears and places them here. And there were so many tears – that they formed this huge ocean... When I came here and heard the sound of the waves, the cry of all the suffering of so many, I can't tell you how much it broke my heart. And at that moment I made a sacred vow: "Master of the World, I swear to you by Your Holy Name that I will not move from this place until You have mercy on your people, until you turn all the pain to joy."

'My dear friend,' said the holy Rebbe, 'I will never leave this Ocean until God has wiped away all of the tears.'

(Lamed Vav, Tzlotana Barbara Midlo, 2004, p.369)

Vorker states,

"Finally, I came out of the forest and found myself on the shore of the sea, an ocean so big I couldn't see the other side."

Do we see this Ocean in Scripture?

> *"Your love, Oh Lord, reaches to the heavens, your faithfulness to the skies. Your righteousness is like the mighty mountain, your justice like the great ocean. Oh Lord, you preserve man and beast... Therefore, the children of men put their trust under the shadow of your wings." (Psalms 36:5-7)*

I have always been puzzled on what Psalm 36:5-7 could mean? *"The Lord's righteousness is like a mighty mountain, Your justice like the great ocean."* Could this verse be speaking about the Mountain of the Lord above and inside the cave it leads to the Ocean of Tears where the Lord's justice is seen in bringing redemptive answers? I believe so...

It is here that our tears on earth (once we are born in the earth) appear and are collected and where tears of intercession and love gather and over time "form" into precious stones in the pool/ocean. Some tears are collected into bottles for spiritual battles and others that have formed into precious stones are mounted in a Wall of Remembrance.

> *"I will give them in My house and within My walls, a memorial and a name better than that of sons and daughters. I will give them an everlasting name that will not be cut off." (Isaiah 56;5)*

This is the heavenly wailing wall made of stones. With the precious stones mounted in it the wall in heaven is the heavenly copy of the "Wailing Wall" of the temple on earth. Jewish tradition says that every morning, drops of dew can be seen on its stones, and it was said that at night the Wall was crying. They say women collected the tears of the Wall as precious remedies for many aliments, spiritual remedies."

> *"You keep track of my wanderings and my weeping. You have stored my many tears in your bottle - not one will be lost. For they are recorded in your book." (Psalm 56:8)*[23]

The Talmud says, "whoever sheds tears at the death of a good man, the Holy One counts them and stores them away in His treasure House."

> *"O you afflicted one, tossed with tempest and not comforted, behold I will lay your stones with colourful gems, And lay your foundations with sapphires. I will make your pinnacles of rubies, your gates of crystal, and your walls of precious stones."*
> *(Isaiah 54:54;11-12)*

Tears are intrinsic to prayer, as it says in the Talmud: "From the day that the Temple was destroyed the gates of prayer have been closed… but even though the gates of prayer are closed, the gates of tears are not closed." The gates of the earthly Temple may be no more, but the prayers of tears are free and ascend up to God's throne to be stored and bottled.

---

[23] Wendy Alec in her book Visions of Heaven, also reveals the glass canisters of tears in her heavenly encounter, "The Father picked up the most exquisitely cut-glass canister filled to the brim with liquid. "These are your tears that you shed during your time of intense trial.' He picked up another much, much larger canister. 'And, these are the tears that I shed, For you, 'And the Father lifted the canister of His tears and poured them over the blood seeping from my heart. Instantly the blood stopped flowing, and a great comfort washed over my heart." (Visions of Heaven, Warboys Publishing, 2013, p.25.)

These bottles of tears are used by God to engulf deliverance in warfare.

> *The Lord's eyes keep on roaming throughout the earth, looking for those whose hearts completely belong to him, so that he may strongly support them.*
> *(2 Chronicles 16:9)*
>
> *"The righteous cry out, and the Lord hears them, He delivers them from all of their troubles." (Psalm 34:17)*
>
> *"Hear my prayer, O God, give ear to my outcry; to my tears be not silent." (Psalms 39:13)*

As on earth before battle the officers were called to pour oil on their weapons (shields). In heaven the angels take often our bottled tears and pour them on their weapons to fight for our deliverances. It's interesting to note that our tears contain oil[24] and they use them above as anointing oil to fuel power for their weapons and our victories.[25]

In Isaiah 21, for example, the prophet is sounding an alarm to Babylon and he cries out, '*Get up, you officers, oil the shields!*' (Is 21:5b, NIV)[26]

---

[24] Tears are created in lacrimal glands in the upper outside corners of your eyes. They're mostly salt and water. **This fluid moves across your eyes as you blink and is mixed with oil from your meibomian glands to form your tears.**

[25] For the weapons of our warfare are not carnal but mighty in God for pulling down strongholds, casting down arguments and every high thing that exalts itself against the knowledge of God, bringing every thought into captivity to the obedience of Christ, and being ready to punish all disobedience when your obedience is fulfilled. (2 Corinthians 10:4-6 NKJV)

[26] Forest House (Isaiah 22:8) - The armoury was held in a forest house just like above where the weapons are held inside the forest cave in the Fathers Garden house (sanctuary). The armoury was designed with three rows according to the

This speaks to our tears that they speak, they speak before God, and they are not silent in the sense they cry out in the Ocean of Tears in heaven. Tears that come from sorrow, but also intercession and heart felt prayers.

As our tears fall from our eyes from the hiddenness of our soul's vibration of pain, they run down our face and to many they just disappear lost in the earth, but in reality, they appear hidden before God, collected and stored.

It is the depth of sincerity indicated by the tears that penetrates the heavenly area under the throne near the Fathers Garden.

Not only do our tears appear in this Ocean, but God, Jesus, also goes to this ocean pool and intercedes for us letting his heart felt tears of love also fall into the Ocean. Tears hold spiritual power.

> *"He is able to save to the uttermost those who come to God through him, since he always lives to make intercession for them." (Hebrews 7:25)*

Isaiah 63:9 says, *"In all their troubles, He was troubled."* - Here we see a God that feels our struggles.

Rabbi Shapira says, "God weeps in His innermost chamber," and backs this up with scripture,

---

Septuagint. It has been suggested that the House of the Forest of Lebanon followed the tripartite layout of the Temple above. The Hall of the Pillars correspond to the Porch (opening), the Forest Chamber to the Holy Place (the Garden), and the Hall of Judgment to the Holy of Holies (Eden).

> *"For if you will not heed, My inmost self must weep in secret, because of your arrogance." (Jeremiah 13:17a)*

God goes on to say,

> *"My eyes will weep bitterly and run down with tears, because the Lord's flock has been taken captive." (Jeremiah 13:17b)*

A Jewish Midrash says, that God's tears flow down his fingers into an ocean pool that builds spiritual power to be released on the earth.

Another Jewish Midrash says, When God sees a suffering child, He drops two tears into an ocean. When it hits the ocean, the sound is so powerful that you can hear it all around.

A friend of mine has seen this ocean pool in their heaven encounters,

"I have seen the place where our tears have been collected in reflecting glass jars of all sizes. The Lord takes me there when He wants me to sit and listen to what's on His heart. I've been numerous times when I was concerned about someone at the campus. Sometimes, He shows me a bottle and tells me why they were shed. We pray together over the situation, and He sends angels to answer the persons prayers. There is a huge body of water, like a lake, that is called the 'tears pool.' It is where our tears are collected when we cry out to God in intercession for others. The angels told me that Jesus' tears are also in this pool. They are added when He walks through the valleys by our side and cries with us. Jesus taught me how the tears in bottles are incredibly powerful, how they are used by the angels for spiritual warfare, and how some turn into extraordinary gems after our prayers have been answered. Those sparkling gems are placed into a special wall so exquisite; I couldn't help but be moved. Especially knowing these tears have come from someone

weeping in pain. I will never think negatively about my tears again."²⁷

Every individual tear is a drop in the ocean full of emotion, holding a feeling and memory encased in vibration. In the heavenly Ocean of Tears under the throne our tears cry out, one can hear them wail and transform into stones.

> *"Then I heard what seemed to be the voice of a great multitude, like the roar of many waters and like the sound of mighty pearls of thunder, crying out."* (Revelation 19:6)

There are also Greek stories of which tears become costly stones[28], and also Jewish.

The Testament of Abraham is a pseudepigraphic text of the Old Testament. Probably composed in the 1st or 2nd century AD, it is of Jewish origin and is usually considered to be part of the apocalyptic literature. It is regarded as scripture by Beta Israel Ethiopian Jews, but not by any other Jewish or Christian groups.

It reads,

> *"3. And as they went on from the field toward his house, beside that way there stood a cypress tree, and by the command of the Lord the tree cried out with a human voice, saying, Holy, holy, holy is the Lord God that calls himself to those that love him; but Abraham hid the mystery, thinking that the chief-captain had not heard the voice of the tree. And coming near to the house they sat down in the court, and Isaac seeing the face*

---

[27] Angela Curtis, Talk With Me in Paradise, Kin & Kingdoms Publishing, 2019, p.83
[28] Greeks and Romans believed the stones were sacred, seeing them as tears of the gods. It is said that after emerging victorious, **Zeus** wept tears which turned to beautiful opals upon hitting the ground.

of the angel said to Sarah his mother, My lady mother, behold, the man sitting with my father Abraham is not a son of the race of those that dwell on the earth. And Isaac ran, and saluted him, and fell at the feet of the Incorporeal, and the Incorporeal blessed him and said, The Lord God will grant you his promise that he made to your father Abraham and to his seed, and will also grant you the precious prayer of your father and your mother. Abraham said to Isaac his son, My son Isaac, draw water from the well, and bring it me in the vessel, that we may wash the feet of this stranger, for he is tired, having come to us from off a long journey. And Isaac ran to the well and drew water in the vessel and brought it to them, and Abraham went up and washed the feet of the chief captain Michael, and the heart of Abraham was moved, and he wept over the stranger. And Isaac, seeing his father weeping, wept also, and the chief captain, seeing them weeping, also wept with them, and the tears of the chief captain fell upon the vessel into the water of the basin and became precious stones. And Abraham seeing the marvel, and being astonished, took the stones secretly, and hid the mystery, keeping it by himself in his heart."

The Chief Captain, the Lord, his tears turned into precious stones. This is very interesting as earlier discussed the Ocean of Tears under the throne is where our tears turn into precious stones. There are even tear drop gemstones that are manifesting in the earth from heaven from people's intercession prayers and tears.

Jesus Christ is the captain of the Host of the Lord in the Old Testament book of Joshua. Christ is our victorious savior, the messenger, angel of the covenant.

In a collection of Islamic stories compiled by Dr. G. Weil, we read the following[29],

---

[29] https://eragem.com/news/the-gemstone-legends-of-ceylon-sri-lanka/

"Adam shed such an abundance of tears that all beasts and birds satisfied their thirst therewith; but some of them sunk into the earth, and, as they still contained some of the juices of his food in Paradise, produced the most fragrant trees and spices. Eve also was desolate in Djidda, for she did not see Adam, although he was so tall that his head touched the lowest heaven, and the songs of the angels were distinctly audible to him. She wept bitterly, and her tears, which flowed into the ocean, were changed into costly pearls, while those which fell on the earth brought forth all beautiful flowers."[30]

It's believed that Adam lived on the slopes of the mountain now known as "Adams Peak". While he cried out to God seeking forgiveness, it is also believed that his tears were transformed into the dazzling gems in the area.

We don't follow Islam, but they must have got their interpretation from somewhere and most likely from Jewish thought.

A Rabbi says; It comforts me because it tells me that there is a place where tears go when they dry; the tears of my infant, the tears of my toddler, the tears of my wife, the tears of my mother, my father, my sister, my friends, myself. These tears are precious things, and there can be no more appropriate destination for them than the Sea of Tears. - (Tears dry and form into precious stones).

Tears are made up of salt mostly, and when salt dry s it turns into stones. Earthly salt stones might not be valued, but tears are precious and they dry in heaven as precious stones in the Ocean of Tears.

The legend of Sinbad's journey in Ceylon,

---

[30] Weil, Dr. G. *The Bible, The Koran, and the Talmud; or, Biblical Legends of the Mussulmans.* New York: 1863.

"As the days wore on, Fortune turned her back upon the stranded sailors. The looming mountain, which spanned the entire coastline, proved a forbidding barrier. Its crystalline slopes, brilliant with the blue of sapphire and the red of rubies, were completely impassible. The only river ran against the grain; drawing from the sea, it flowed into the bowels of a dark and imposing cave into the belly of the mountain. After days on end with no hope of escape, their gaunt and hope-starved bodies began to fall one by one upon the sands of this unforgiving shore."[31]

This is an interesting story as it almost sounds like the knowledge of the Fathers Garden under the throne through the cave to an ocean of precious stones. The story goes on to say of - Sinbad's sister; Tears flowed from her eyes and become red and green jewels. Sinbad gathers the jewels faster and faster and runs through the cavern.

Another Jewish Midrash, says that tears were God's gift, a sign of His love for Adam and Eve after they were banished from the Garden of Eden. Who wouldn't cry leaving that garden having to tough it out in the world? The first couple would face inevitable sorrows and difficulties. God said, "For this reason I give you out of My heavenly treasure this priceless pearl. Look! It is a tear! And when grief overtakes you and your heart aches so that you are not able to endure it, and great anguish grips your soul, then there will fall from your eyes this tiny tear. Then your burden will grow lighter."[32]

---

[31] Sindbad's Voyage, and other Oriental Fictions, is particularly considered, *London Review*, February 1799, p. 105-107.

[32] In recent times for many - precious stones have been created in heaven to then manifest on earth due to the precious tears people have cried. Tear drop looking stones, the residue of answered prayers. A token of their heart.

Conclusions – We have seen that precious stones 'arc' off into the river of life turning it into the Crystal Sea. That there are two types of categories for the stones 1, Our existence and 2, Spiritual physical tokens of God's creative works. We have seen that Jewish Rabbis know of a place called the Ocean of Tears of which our tears appear and can form into precious stones and be mounted into the "Wall of Remembrance" or be collected and stored in tear bottles for the angels to use in warfare over our redemption battles.

We have also seen that others have seen this place in heaven encounters more recently[33]. The concept of tears turning into precious stones is seen in the Bible, in Jewish, Greek, and Islamic traditions and in other legends.

---

[33] My friend who has seen much of heaven in their encounters first shared of this place called the Ocean of Tears (pool of tears). It was only after intense research that I found Rabbi's confirmation. My friend had no other knowledge of the Ocean other than their experiences.

The Four Rivers
of the Crystal Sea

The fours rivers that divide from the crystal sea continue down the Mountain until they flow into Eden and into Adam's garden. In the first river, which is called "Pishon", there is gold and precious stones. These came down from the throne to earth, through the spiritual river/realm.

> *"A river flows out of Eden to water the garden, and from there it divides and becomes four branches. The name of the first is Pishon; it is the one that flows around the whole land of Havilah, where there is gold; and the gold of that land is good; bdellium and onyx stone are there."*[34] *(Genesis 2:10)*

Adam was the first king and priest and would have had to have gone up to the "Mountain of God" to the throne of God. I don't believe he stood their naked, like a cave man, but more likely clothed with a robe of light, glory, and covered with jewels.[35]

Adam was considered to be a priest serving God in the sanctuary of Eden. The book of Jubilees (160 BC) represents an

---

[34] The onyx stones decorated both the tabernacle and temple, as well as the high priestly garments (Exod. 25:7; 28:9-12, 20; 1 Chr. 29:2). Gold and onyx are also found together on the priests clothing (Exod. 28:6-27) and mentioned together as composing parts of the temple (1 Chr. 29:2).

[35] While sin and disobedience had not yet come on the scene, they were clad in that glory from above which caused them no shame. But after the breaking of the law, then entered the scene both shame and awareness of their nakedness. (Louth, Conti and Oden, Ancient Christian Commentary on Scripture: Old Testament I, Genesis 1-11 2001, 72)

early Jewish interpretation of Adam as a priest in an arboreal temple.

There is a Jewish Midrash that says; Adam was given a book in the garden of Eden. And because there was no written parchment, it was engraved on a sapphire stone. As Adam held it up to his eyes, a flame burned inside and took the form of the letters, so Adam could read.[36]

---

[36] B. Avodah Zarah 5a.

The Wilderness

Jewish tradition in Rabbinical literature says, that Moses departed from the heavens with two tablets on which the ten commandments were engraved, and they were made of sapphire like stone (Legends of the Jews).

The Sapphire, used for the tablets was taken from the throne of glory. Again, we see heaven stones coming to earth[37].

One Jewish Commentary says, speaking about the Urim and Thummim stones, which hid inside the breastplate of the high priest, and communicated the Lord's will and lit up with a message,

"The Urim and Thummim did not belong in the physical world, they were not from this world. Nachmanides, likewise describes the stones in parchment as the handiwork of heaven, and a secret handed to Moses from the mouth of the Almighty."[38]

Rabbi Ari Enkin, Rabbinic Director of the United with Israel; says,

"For those unfamiliar, there were very few grocery stores, restaurants and bakeries in the Sinai desert back then (and today

---

[37] Moses and the leaders were told to go up into the heavenly mountain "And they saw the God of Israel. There was under his feet as it were a pavement of sapphire stone, like the very heaven for clearness. (Exodus 24:10). Moses and the rest of Israel's leadership were given the profound privilege of seeing God. The LORD said to Moses, "Come up to me on the mountain and wait there, that I may give you the tablets of stone, with the law and the commandment, which I have written for their instruction." (Exodus 24:12) The tablets were made of sapphire.

[38] Rabbi Dovid Rosenfeld, (n.d.) Urim and Thummim.
http://www.aish.com/atr/Urim-and-Thummim.html

too!). But the more than one million Jewish people had to eat during the 40 years of wandering in the desert. So, God sent manna down from heaven each day (except on Shabbat), which was a bread like food that sustained them."*

Not many people know this, but the Midrash (rabbinic literature) teaches that along with the daily allotted loaf of manna came… jewellery! That's right. The manna was accompanied by diamonds and other precious stones. Now get this; The Midrash continues by saying "the greatest" people (referring to the leaders) went right for the jewels, while "the simple folk" cared about the manna.

Rabbi Michel Twerski of Milwaukee says "The financial and economic situation of the Jewish people in the desert was very unique; they had no needs. Everything was taken care off. Their food fell from heaven. They were accompanied by "Miriam's well," which provided fresh water at all times. Their clothing never wore out. There was no disease or illness. God ensured that the weather was always comfortable. If one has no needs or expenses, then what was the use of the precious stones? Who would trade them? Where were they to be deposited? What would they be used to buy? Indeed, it may very well be that ultimately, the precious stones were completely useless! Precious stones in the deserts would have about as much value as sand in a desert or snow in the Artic.

The answer, is explained, is that "great people" see far beyond the here and now. The "great people" knew, or were at least anticipating, that one day there would be a Mishkan (Tabernacle) and a Beit Hamilkdash (Holy Temple), where a High Priest would need precious stones as part of his breastplate. These leaders were not collecting the precious stones due to some kind of materialistic obsession. Rather, they were collecting due to their sensitivity to the spiritual needs of a nation.

This account also appears in the Midrash (Shemot Rabba 33;8), which adds that "the leaders among them would come and collect them and hide them." The "gedolim," the prominent members of the nation, collected these precious jewels and hide them until they were needed for the priestly garments. The Yefei Toar commentary to the Midrash explains this to mean that the precious stones fell only with the portions of manna intended for these prominent individuals and this is why only they collected the jewels. Alternatively, the Yefei Toar suggests, Moshe (Moses) perhaps issued a specific directive authorizing only these leaders to collect the precious stones."[39]

Why did the Jewels fall in the wilderness? Because God was betrothing his bride, his community in beauty. Can there be a bridal canopy without a bride?

> *"I will greatly rejoice in the Lord, my soul shall be joyful in my God. For He has clothed me with the garments of salvation, He has covered me with the robe of righteousness, as a bridegroom decks himself with ornaments, and as a bride adorns herself with her jewels." (Isaiah 61:10)*
>
> *"Does a young woman forget her jewellery, a bride her wedding ornaments? Yet my people have forgotten me, days without number." (Jeremiah 2:23)*

---

[39] Rabbi Ari Enkin, (2015 January), *Living Torah: Leaving Egypt and Looking to the Future*, http://Unitedwithisrael.org/living-torah-leaving-egypt-and-looking-to-the-future/

Professor G. K. Beale from Westminister Theological Seminary says, "According to tradition, precious stones fell along with the manna."[40] (Midrash Psalm 78:4)

The Catholic Scholar Stephen Beale says, "Moreover, according to ancient Jewish tradition, precious stones and pearls rained down from heaven along with the manna."[41]

The Targum Yonason says, "that heavenly clouds brought the stones from the Pishon River to the wilderness."

Yoma 75a:19, a treatise in the Mishnah and Talmud, says,

"With regards to donations for the tabernacle, the verse states, and they brought yet to him freewill offerings every morning (Exodus 36:3) - What is the meaning of every morning? This teaches that pearls and precious stones fell for the Israelites with the manna. Its states, and the rulers brought the onyx stones."

The Midrash Exodus Rabb, chapter 33 says, - "Along with the manna which fell for Israel in the desert and provided them sustenance, precious stones and Jewels fell. The leaders of Israel came and gathered them and stored them for the tabernacle."

> *"I will give you hidden treasures, riches stored in secret places, so that you may know that I AM the Lord, the God of Israel, who summons you by name."*
> *(Isaiah 45:3)*

Rabbi Bloch recounts a Midrash, The Midrash talks about Rabbi Shimon Ben Hal-Phta who was really impoverished and prayed to God to provide him wealth. A part of a hand came

---

[40] G.K.Beale, *The Book of Revelation: A Commentary on the Greek Text.* Grand Rapids: Paternoster Press, 1999, p.252-253.
[41] Stephen Beale, (Nov 2017) *Why do Christians Get White Stones in Heaven?*

down from the heavens and gave him a precious stone. Rabbi Shimon sold it and brought provision for the Sabbath (Midrash Tehillim 92)

In the **Testament of Solomon**, a work of the 1st to 2nd century, it describes the angel Michael giving Solomon a powerful ring from Heaven, with an engraved precious stone on it.

Now, yes angels can bring the stones down through the veil to earth this is a very common way the stones manifest. Especially throughout people's houses. In recent times precious stones have appeared in jewellery from angels bringing them down from heaven and placing them through the veil.

Michael C. King in his book, *Gemstones from Heaven*, who has received thousands of little stones in meetings and houses gives a testimony of some stones appearing in settings and even a pendant,

> "Rarer still, probably close to one in five thousand gems or more, will be a stone that appears in a setting of some kind. This can be a ring, cuff links, pendent, or earrings. On at least one occasion that I know of, the chain even appeared with the pendent."[42]

Conclusions - We have seen that Jewish tradition describes that heavenly stones came down to earth. First in the garden with Adam and Eve and then out of the clouds of God's presence in the wilderness. The stones in the wilderness were for the Priests functions and also to represent the Temple. Spiritually that is pointing to "US" as the true living stones (a stone in the true

---

[42] Michael C. King, *Gemstones From Heaven*, Self Published, 2016, p. 10

Temple - Jesus) coming down to earth to tabernacle [43]. The heavenly stones that fell in the wilderness were used for the building of the material Sanctuary (Temple) as a shadow of things to come. Jewish traditions also speak of precious stones coming down by angels in jewellery.

> *"Who serve the copy and shadow of the heavenly things, as Moses was divinely instructed when he was about to make the tabernacle. For He said, "See that you make all things according to the pattern shown you on the mountain." (Hebrews 8:5)*

---

[43] When we were born into the earth our spirit was sent from above like a precious stone. I explain our pre-existence in my book, *Pre-existence: The Hidden Mystery*.

Jesus Adorns the Bride – 33AD

In the Old Testament in the wilderness, while precious stones fell God was leading, comforting and encouraging His people His bride to journey with Him and walk with Him. So, we should ask does Jesus adorn His bride? Jesus said,

> *"And if I go and prepare a place for you, I will come again and receive you to Myself, that where I am, there you may be also. And where I go, you know, and the way." (John 14:1-4)*

In ancient Jewish culture, when they became betrothed a gold coin or jewels were given and the bridegroom went away for twelve months, the jewels were a reminder of His love (Genesis 24:53).

The price paid by the father of the groom to the father of the bride was called *mohar*. (The term continues to be included in the text of the traditional *ketubah*, or Jewish wedding contract.) In Genesis (Parashat Vayishlah), Shekhem [Dinah's suitor] said to Dinah's father and her brothers: "Let me find favor in your eyes, and what ye shall say unto me I will give. Ask me never so much mohar and mattan, and I will give according as ye shall say unto me; but give me the damsel to wife."

Mattan was the Hebrew word for the gifts given by the groom to the bride in addition to the mohar.

The *mohar* was not always paid in cash. Sometimes it was paid in kind, or in service. The Book of Genesis relates the story of the servant of Abraham, who, after his request for Rebecca [to marry Isaac] was granted, "brought forth jewels of silver, and jewels of gold, and raiment, and gave them to Rebecca; he gave also to her brother and to her mother precious things." The servant thus gave *mattan* to Rebecca, and *mohar* to her brother and mother.[44]

If we spiritualise the Jewish culture, the father of the groom is God (Father), and the bridegroom is Jesus. The Father chose us, all believers to marry Jesus. Therefore, Jesus as the bridegroom goes away to prepare a place for us the bride. When the bridegroom came to collect his bride, he would adorn her with jewels then take her to his father's house to be with him forever. The bridegroom collecting his bride is Jesus leading us through life, our wilderness, and bringing us into the Fathers presence and house in heaven. And it is along this journey that we are adorned with jewels.[45]

> *"I delight greatly in the LORD; my soul rejoices in my God. For he has clothed me with garments of salvation and arrayed me in a robe of his righteousness, as a bridegroom adorns his head like a priest, and as a bride adorns herself with her jewels." (Isaiah 61:10)*

Conclusions – As in the garden, the wilderness, the revelation continues to unfold in the New Testament with Jesus. As the true Temple (Jesus as the head), we being part of His body, He is transforming us in holiness and betrothing us with love gifts.

---

[44] https://www.myjewishlearning.com/article/ancient-jewish-marriage/

[45] Ian Clayton in his book "Realms of the Kingdom, Volume Two", says,"When the son or daughter of a Hebrew family married a Gentile, after the bride and bridegroom had come out of the huppah, they would take diamond, gold and sapphire dust and throw it over the bride and bridegroom as the power of endowment and their acceptance and sanctification of marriage. Did you wonder why gold, diamonds, sapphires and precious stones are showing up?"

> *"For I feel a divine jealousy for you, since I betrothed you to one husband, to present you as a pure virgin to Christ." (2 Corinthians 11:2)*

> *"For as the body is one, and hath many members, and all the members of that one body, being many, are one body: so also, is Christ." (1 Corinthians 12:12)*

As we are walking through the earth being tested and polished, (fashioned) we are being transformed ready to dwell in our spiritual Temple home, and our "works" are being tested (1 Cor 3:12)[46]. We each will have an area, a dwelling place as part of the heavenly Temple/city.

We were the Temple bride in heaven before we were sent into the earth.

Temples in the Ancient Near East were generally constructed from stone blocks. Aven, the Hebrew word for stone, is formed from two words; Av (father) and ben (son). Ben also comes from the root word 'banah' which means to build. The Father through the Son, brought forth the mystery and built the spiritual house from precious stones for which we are (1 Peter 2:5). All God's children came forth in the light, we came out of the rock (Christ), out of the heavenly earth's Temple as precious stones and we were engraved, weaved and knitted together as spirit beings. We were made in the lowest parts of the earth, the netherworld, the other-word above, but under God's throne in the cave of His womb drawn up before the altar.

And we will be the heavenly Temple in the future in heaven.

---

[46] Our works ultimately show forth the nature of our hearts.

Apostle John – Book of Revelation – 95AD

John had knowledge of believers receiving from heaven, manna and a white stone inscribed with a new name on it.

> *"He who has an ear, let him hear what the spirit says to the churches. To him who overcomes I will give some of the hidden manna to eat. And I will give him a white stone, and on the stone a new name written which no one knows except him who receives it." (Rev 2:17)*

Dr. Eli Lizorkin Eyzenberg says, regarding the white stone Jesus gives overcomer's,

> *"The white stone was given to overcomers of a trail, as a victory stone in ancient times. A white stone of acquittal. Another suggestion the white stones with names of the recipients inscribed, were given to contest winners of the Roman sport races."*[47]

This white victory stone given to believers when they reach heaven, offers insight to believers today who are receiving manifested victory stones after great trails. These stones are a foretaste to the ultimate white stone believers will receive at the end of the race.

A white stone was also used to gain admission to certain events in Roman times. That would imply that those who overcome will be granted admission to the Kingdom and greater realms.

---

[47] Dr. Eli Lizorkin Eyzenberg from https://israelbiblicalstudies.com/bible-jewish- studies/#bible-studies

Early Church Fathers Interpretations

- Hippolytus of Rome, (early 3rd century) for example, wrote that "The white stone is the teaching which a bishop imparts to the faithful immediately after their baptism and which must not be revealed before." (*Apostolic Tradition* 23)
- Victorinus of Pettau, (late 3rd century) on the other hand, took a much different approach to this passage, explaining that "The white gem is adoption to be the son of God; the new name written on the stone is 'Christian.'" (*Commentary on the Apocalypse*) Jerome agreed with this interpretation. (*Homily 25 on the Psalms*)
- Both Caesarius of Arles (late 5th to early 6th century) and the Venerable Bede (late 6th to early 7th century) understood the white quality of the stone to be directly related to baptism, and that the name related to our calling as "sons of God." (*Commentary on Revelation* and *The Explanation of the Apocalypse*)
- Andrew of Caesarea (late 6th to early 7th century) believed this *"new name"* would not be known until the world to come, as he writes, "And they will receive both the small white stone, that is, the victorious being deemed worthy of the right portion, and the new name which is unknown in the present life." (*Commentary*)

As there is a warning to believers that the stone is given to them who overcome, I believe Andrew of Caesarea is right that it is dependent on if you are deemed worthy, have walked worthy to be not just a dweller in heaven but a member of the city[48].

---

[48] "But in a great house there are not only vessels of gold and silver, but also of wood and clay, some for honor and some for dishonor. Therefore if anyone cleanses himself from the latter, he will be a vessel for honor, sanctified and useful for the Master, prepared for every good work." (2 Timothy 2:20-21) - And our good works will be like 'precious stones'.

Meaning and Purposes, Sizes and Colours

God is creative and every stone has a meaning and function. Some for spiritual positions (of authority) such as walking in the role of a Priest, and King, and also as part of the Bride. Others are the out workings of spiritual works. There are different grades of stones, some precious and others just little gem tokens of no real earthly value (but of spiritual value).

> *"Now I have prepared with all my might for the house of my God the gold for things to be made of gold, and the silver for things of silver, and the brass for things of brass, the iron for things of iron, and wood for things of wood; onyx stones, and stones to be set, glistering stones, and of divers colours." (1 Chronicles 29:2)*

Many of the stones appearing are semi-precious. Many just look like glassy stones. Scripture calls these glistening stones. That is not to say that diamonds, rubies and emeralds have not appeared because they have.

Thousands of stones fall behind the spiritual veil and sit behind our earthly world around our lives building a spiritual frequency. But many also in these days are coming through the veil manifesting as physical stones one can hold.

There are different sizes, colours and functions. Blue can mean the out working of an open heaven, clear can mean answered prayers, and green can mean the out working of healing on creation, and burgundy can mean international travelling (ministry[49]) angels[50]. Others are the residue of answered prayers or a promise to hold on to in a difficult season when we walk in valleys or storms[51]. The stones can also be just a sign and wonder, there is a token (stone) that can represent just about any spiritual truth or out working.

The stones are not only beautiful, but they also worship with their own colour and sound, and emit their own emotion.[52] They are living stones.

---

[49] "Are they not all ministering spirits sent forth to minister for those who will inherit salvation." (Hebrews 1:14)
[50] Angela Curtis, Explore With Me In Paradise, Kin & Kingdom Publishing, 2023, p.129
[51] Angela Curtis, p. 99
[52] Angela Curtis, , p. 90

Gold and Money Appears!

"The silver is mine, and the gold is mine, says the Lord of hosts." (Haggai 2:8)

"Go to the sea, and cast in a hook, and that fish which shall first come up, take, and when thou has opened its mouth, thou shall find a coin, take it and give it to them for me and thee (Matthew 17:26)

St. Benedict (543 AD) – had a disciple who was heavily burdened with debt. The man was constantly being harassed for the debt. St. Benedict felt his sorrow and told him to come back in 3 days. Benedict spent the 3 days in deep prayer. On his return he told the disciple to go and inspect a store of grain. He went and discovered thirteen gold pieces lying on top of the grain, a gift from God to pay the debt.

St. Dominic (1170 AD) - As he never took money with him, he had to ask free passage across ferries. On one occasion the boatman refused to ferry him across without his fare, so he lifted his eyes to heaven, prayed and found at his feet the required money.

St. Lydwine (1433 AD) - She went to pay some bills, she placed some money in the purse, and gave her purse to her cousin, Nicolas. He paid the bills and returned the purse to her. Although she knew the money was gone, she turned it over. Out fell eight coins, the exact amount she had given her cousin to pay the debts of her brother. After seeing the miraculous supply of money, she decided that the purse should be called the purse of Jesus. It is said that the saint could always draw upon it for needs of the poor. It did not become exhausted, since even on the day of her death it was still full.

We see here that God can provide money, gold and a purse that never runs out. I know of people who have received small junks of gold, and also gems-encrusted with gold casing around them. These stone have appeared in the hand of children while in trances/visions, while they are encountering heaven. I also have a friend who has lived for the past 12 years with an open purse from the Lord. When money is needed, they pray, then put their hand in their pocket and the money is there and if there is any change, as soon as it goes back in the pocket it disappears.

Just like St. Lydwine and her purse there are others who have pockets that are heavenly ATM machines.

One of my friends walks in this reality,

On one of my adventures to New Zealand, my friend Mandy and I were driving from the airport when we spotted a sign to a strawberry farm. neither of us had money, but we both craved strawberries. We prayed and followed the signs to the farm kiosk. After we chose two of the best-looking strawberries chips, I smiled at Mandy as I put my hand into my pocket. Some paper was there.
When I pulled out my hand, I was holding a crisp New Zealand twenty-dollar bill. We laughed, bought the strawberries and carried them to the car. I put the change back in my pocket. When reached our destination, strawberries eaten, my pocket was empty. Just as the money appeared, the change disappeared. The following week, Jase, Chris, Jesse and I were on our way to a holiday house. We didn't have any provisions for the weekend, so we decided we'd stop. and get some. 'Here's my Visa card, Jan,' Jase said smiling. 'Go get some munchies.'
'Don't worry, the Lord will provide,' I said as I checked my pockets. They were empty, but I knew the Lord would provide. He always did, but not before it was needed. We all walked

around the supermarket and filled our trolley. When we arrived at the counter, Chris and Jess unloaded the food while I prayed. 'That's forty-eight dollars and twenty cents,' the checkout lady said. I pulled a fresh fifty-dollar bill from my pocket. The Lord had miraculously provided again. The Lord has continued to supply my daily needs this way for many years.[53]

God also has bank accounts in the earth which He shifts money around the world. How this is done is a bit of a mystery, but I have some insights on how it unfolds,

* Money can be provided supernaturally and people pay the money into bank accounts, that He (God) has set up around the world through other people. Then the Lord transfers it to whom He wills (internet banking).

* Angels can morph into human form and pay money into bank accounts - "Be not forgetful to entertain strangers, for thereby some have entertained angels unawares." (Hebrews 13:2)

* The Lord himself can walk into banks morphed in human disguise and pay money in or use ATM cards. Jesus did this in the Bible - "After that, He appeared in another "form" to two of them as they walked and went into the country." (Mark 16:12) - "Who are you seeking? She supposed Him to be the gardener." (John 20:14). Yes, Jesus does visit the earth...

Some may say, "but for the money to be legal it must be already circulating in the earth with government serial numbers. For it can't just be created out-side the system, so where does the money come from?"

---

[53] Angela Curtis, p. 96

The answer:

All around the world in Churches people put money into offering bags. This money is given unto the Lord. Therefore, the Lord supernaturally takes the money from the bags before it is counted and shifts it to other places and into hands to either use or bank[54].

---

[54] The Lord collects the money on a Sunday, stores it in a safe place (cash bunker on earth). Then translocates the money and materialises it as it is needed into peoples pockets. Angels can also drop money into our pockets as well.

Mystical Jewellery!
The Mystics!

In my previous book, *Wilderness Like Eden*, I documented extensively the supernatural phenomenon of gemstones appearing as gifts from heaven. This phenomenon I documented from a Jewish, Old Testament witness, and from what is recorded in Rabbinical Commentaries. But since the publication of that book, I have discovered new accounts through Church history, of Saints receiving heavenly Jewellery from members of the Godhead.

Throughout Church History, this phenomenon has been related many times to the term "Mystical espousal", which leads to Mystical marriage. In these encounters, members of the Godhead, mainly Jesus appear and give a heavenly ring or other heavenly gifts or jewellery to believers. These rings and jewels are from heaven and are clearly seen by those who wear them and by others. But sometimes, the rings are only seen be the one who has received them as they stay behind the veil, but are always there on the finger.

This mystical process is a bit like being called as a single one in the Kingdom, total devoted to Jesus with great intimacy.

St. John of the Cross explains the difference between the espousal and the marriage,

> *"In the espousal there is only a mutual agreement and willingness between the two, and the bridegroom graciously gives jewels and ornaments to his espoused. But the marriage there is also a communication and union between the persons. Although the bridegroom sometimes visits the bride in the*

espousal and brings her presents, as we said, there is no union of persons. Spiritual marriage is incomparably greater than the spiritual espousal, for it is a total transformation in the Beloved in which each surrenders the entire possession of self to the other with a certain consummation of the union of love."[55]

Dr. Imbert Gourbeyre once did a historical study and found close to a 100 people who had experienced the mystical espousal of mystical marriage. Of these encounters 55 had received the mystical rings.

Lucy of Narni, born in Italy in the early 1500s was once in prayer, and there she was given a vision of Jesus, Angels and other Saints. Jesus then espoused her to himself, placing a mystical Heavenly ring on her finger. We see in these accounts that visions are not imaginations, but encounters through the spiritual veil as Lucy received a physical ring. We also see that the Great Cloud of Witnesses is active, ministering with Jesus.

Phillip H. Wiebe mentions the account of Stephana Quinzani, born in Italy 1457 near Brescia,

> *"Christ is said to have appeared to her accompanied by a few Saints... and then espoused himself to her, giving her a ring that was seen by many people. She experienced another encounter sometime later, after renouncing her own will to do the will of God. Jesus appeared to her and said, 'My daughter, since of the love of Me you have generously stripped yourself of your own will, ask what you will, and I will grant it to you.' Her reply was, 'I desire nothing but yourself, O Lord.'"*

Now this is not strange, I have friends who have received jewellery from the Lord, that is earrings, pearls, heart-shaped gemstones, all received in heaven and then manifest in their

---

[55] Joan, Carroll Cruz, Mysteries Marvels & Miracles: In The Lives of The Saints, Tan Books, 1997, p. 142.

hands as they come out of their encounters back on earth. Their bodies stay on earth, while their spirits encounter heaven and the Lord above.

St. Colette (1447 AD) not only received a ring from Jesus, but while in deep prayer in the presence of her community, she was drawn into ecstasy. When she came out of it, she found in her hand a small golden crucifix that had appeared. On one side of the golden crucifix, a blue stone was imprinted, and also a red stone in the middle. Surrounding the red stone, were four pearls fixed, and a large pearl at the bottom of the cross. These two gifts, the ring and the crucifix were seen by many.[56]

Joan Carroll Cruz, in her book, *Mysteries, Marvels, Miracles* in the lives of the Saints, reports,

> *"St. Catherine dei Ricci experienced the mystical espousal. Our saviour appeared to the saint, radiant with light, and drawing from his own finger a gleaming ring, He placed it upon the forefinger of her left hand, saying, My daughter, receive this ring as a pledge and proof that thou dost now, and ever shall belong to Me. Catherine described the ring as being of gold and set with a large pointed diamond...Since the event took place in 1542, and St. Catherine lived another 48 years after the event, there was still alive a number of people who had seen the ring when witnesses were questioned in 1614."*

It is interesting, having seen them myself that jewels manifest from heaven with the same experience of the jewellery (ring) gleaming as if glowing with glory on it. I have seen many gemstones appear supernaturally that glow for a short while, and then over time lose the Presence.

And again,

---

[56] Cruz, p.151.

"St. Veronica Giulinai (1727 AD) - A Capuchin nun. The event took place on April 11, 1694. She received a mystical ring from the hand of Jesus which many witnesses were privileged to see. One witness related, "The ring encircled her ring finger as ordinary rings do, This ring was not always visible, but at times was seen clearly."[57]

St. Jean Marie (1859 AD) - received a ring from Jesus that was clearly witnessed and attested by many.[58]

In 1948 in the ministry of the Golden Candlestick, a group of ladies who spent hours a day in prayer experienced being raptured up into heavenly encounters, sometimes physically being caught up in their bodies and returning with heavenly jewels and gifts and clothing,

James Maloney reports,

"All the earthly translations and raptures were separate from the translations to heaven, where many would return with sandals entwined with strange jewels, vest-like garments inset with twelve stones representing the tribes of Israel, headdresses arrayed in almost living colours, articles of clothing that would be stitched with gold tread - mean the metal, not the colour. These were regular occurrences with the ladies of gold."[59]

These ladies would physically start to be translated and on their return, they were clothed with jewels and clothing.

Maloney goes on to share,

"The ceiling was concealed in a purple, swirling cloud - sometimes feathers were whirling inside the cloud. Out of the

---

[57] Cruz, p.150.
[58] Cruz, p.150.
[59] James Maloney, Ladies of Gold; The Remarkable Ministry of the Golden Candlestick, Answering the Cry Publications, 2011, p. 9.

cloud, one could often hear the audible laughter of exultant children. It truly was an open-heavens, a spiritual portal like Jacobs Ladder. There were numerous times the four and twenty elders were a part of the worship. And just a consistent coming and going of the angelic host. When an angel was there, one could see them like they see a normal human being, fully manifested, no similitude (the outline of an angel). They would come to worship and share information with the group. Often, they wore "normal" clothes. On one occasion I saw two men in street clothes, sitting and conversing with some of the ladies before the service. When the meeting was starting these two stood up and gave hugs to the ladies, then walked past me and disappeared.

I recall once three ladies worshipping in an angelic tongue, whose faces and torsos were concealed behind a purple cloud - all I could see were their arms and hands outstretched. Again, I remember a powerful instance where the roomful of ladies was dancing before the Lord, caught up in the spirit, with their eyes completely shut, yet they never bumped into each other, being perfectly orchestrated by God.

I recall seeing a door in that sanctuary, beautiful moulded, emanating a golden hue. I assumed when people walked through it, it led to another part of the house. Many years later, when walking through the house in the day time with Marion Pickard (Frances personal assistant, and the second to last original member alive beside Dora) I was stunned to realize the door was not there. It was explained to me that door was a special door to heaven. I didn't bother asking further details - they wouldn't have been provided anyway."[60]

These Jewels and gifts were physical, not imaginary, and manifested for them to keep on earth. As I stated earlier, I personally have seen gemstones manifest from heaven, and I have seen children in heavenly trances encounter Jesus, and materialise gemstones in their hands after coming out of their visions. I have also been in the company of children who have

---

[60] James Maloney, p. 10-11

brought down heavenly gifts to give to others, which stay behind the veil. In one occurrence I received a ring and a crown (and other gifts) that were given to me by these children.

In the book, *Talk With Me In Paradise,* by Angela Curtis, it recounts similar encounters of children bringing down rings, crowns and gifts to give people. It is with these children that I encountered my experiences.

One child shares her experience below; these experiences are full-blown heaven visitations,

> *"There are places in Heaven which are full of royal rings and signet rings, and another is full of crowns for all the children. I can store the treasures Jesus gives me in my house. Sometimes, Jesus gives me a crown to give away to someone. I've given crowns to lots of visitors at our campus. I like giving them to Man and Sir the most. All the crowns have beautiful coloured stones set in the gold, but they all look different. When I put them on someone's head, it gives them peace, and they smile a lot. When I put one on, I feel a buzzing go through me like when the Holy Spirit touches me.*
> *"I've even been given small crowns for the children at the Home (these are the ones that stay behind the veil). I was given a ring, golden clothes and gold sandals for one of the visitors who came to the Home. One day, I was given precious stones to give to Mam. All the gifts in Heaven are glowing with light. I love getting heaven treasure, but I love giving them away more."*[61]

---

[61] Angela Curtis; Talk With Me In Paradise; Kin & Kingdom Book, 2019, p.87.

The Prophecy of the Stones in the 1980s

From my research the documentation of when the manifestation of recent gemstones started to appear again, I have been able to pin-point it first to the Ministry of the Golden Candle-Stick Ladies in 1948 and then to a prophecy a man called Glenn Smith received back in the 1980s[62].

I quote,

"Glenn has a remarkable testimony filled with miraculous workings of God. Back in the 1980s, twenty years before the gems began to appear, Glenn received a prophetic word from a humble believer that foretold this manifestation, it's cost and effect on him and others. He did not understand it at the time, but in retrospect, certainty does now. Another time, when Glenn and Terrie were in Jerusalem, Israel in 1996, they had a mysterious encounter with a most unusual jewellery maker and gem dealer that foreshadowed what would begin in their lives a decade later."[63]

It was in 2006 that Glenn Smith started to receive gemstones from heaven, even from Jesus Himself,

"In 2006, I had a very unusual experience and Jesus Himself walked through my living room. In His path, He dropped a beautiful teardrop-shaped gemstone[64]*. The next morning the entire path was littered with tumbled amethysts and lace cut*

---

[62] Glenn Smith was told that many stones would come around his life.

[63] Glenn & Terrie Smith, Gemstones from Heaven, Self- publishing, p. 1

[64] Tear-drop gem; Intercessory/Prayers fulfilled - Tears / Ocean of Tears - formed and manifested on earth.

agates, Over the next nine years, thousands of stones have appeared from Heaven with hundreds of witnesses."[65]

---

[65] Glenn & Terrie Smith, p.2

RUTH WARD HEFLIN

Ruth Heflin was a minister for forty years. She stood before kings and rulers and slept in mud huts preaching the Gospel. She was an anointed prophet and knew how to enter the glory realm. Ruth died in September of 2000. She had given many prophecies. One of the things she prophesied about was the fact that God was going to do three miraculous things. First it would be gold dust. Then it would be gemstones and finally creative miracles of body parts.[66]

---

[66] Heflin was not saying it would be the first time these signs had appeared in history, but that they were about to start again.

Gold Dust and Gold Teeth

Around 1998 flowing from 'Silvania Machado' (at the Toronto Airport Fellowship Church - Pastor John Arnott) and then through the ministry of Ruth Heflin, David Herzog and many others the gold manifestation started to increase around the world. This manifestation is not new its first appearance is thought to have been in the 1980s in Argentina says Chrisma Magazine, but Ruth Heflin records cases of it happening in the revival of the 1960s. She says, "it happened occasionally during the 1970s and 1980s as well."

Heflin says,

> *"The golden glory appears in various unique ways. It comes through the pores of the skin on the face or hands or some other part of the body of those who are worshipping the Lord. It rains down from heaven, falling on either the people, their clothing or their surroundings. I have also watched as the golden glory was being created before my eyes and fell upon people. We have experienced it as rain, as mist and as a cloud of God's presence with us. It is definitely supernatural and can be explained in no other way. It comes on those of us who are ministering, but it also comes on many in the congregation. It comes on people of all ages, even on very small children and babies. Some have even had gold nuggets fall on them"* [67]

Some may think it's all fake, but I have myself experienced gold dust appearing in intense worship meetings in little jungle huts in India in very remote places. I have witnessed it appear on my friends face while teaching. Another friend of mine who went to stay at the Orphanage for a few weeks, on their return to New Zealand woke up first morning back in her bed to find rainbow,

---

[67] Ruth Ward Heflin, Golden Glory, McDougal Publishing, 2000, p. 13

gold, silver dust all over her pillow.[68] This most likely was a manifestation, gift, residue of the glory of God.

From the gold dust manifestation then came the gold teeth miracles.

> *"Some of the people who received this type of miracle were in need of it. With others, God would replace their silver-coloured amalgam fillings with what looked like shiny gold. At first, it happened to one or two, and then it began to happen to many. At first, someone got a single gold filling, but it wasn't long before some were receiving many fillings. In some cases, the person involved had every single filling in their mouth turn to gold. It was awesome to look at, and those who saw it were deeply moved. Many of these miracles were examined by dentists, who confirmed that they were gold and found no way to explain it. It was another of God's signs and wonders to show us how much He loved us."*[69]

Again, this manifestation is not new, church growth expert, C. Peter Wagner, reports that there have been isolated reports of gold fillings in North America even in the late 1800s.[70]

Gold dust, gold nuggets, silver, sapphire dust and even gold teeth have happened all around the world. I recommend the book "Golden Glory; The New Wave of Signs and Wonders" by: Ruth Ward Heflin, where she gives testimony after testimony of these occurrences.

Mehesh Chavda is another one who is living this experience at the present time. Mehesh has done dozens of 40- and 20-day fasts. And just about every time Mehesh preaches a supernatural

---

[68] Siteri Saurara.
[69] Heflin, p.23
[70] Heflin, p. 297

manifestation of gold dust begins to cover his body and comes upon those who are listening.

> *"Then shall thou lay up gold as dust, and the gold of Ophir as the stones of the brooks. Yea, the Almighty shall be thy defence, and thou shalt have plenty of silver." (Job 22:24-25)*

> *"Though ye lien among the sheepfolds, You are the wings of a dove covered with silver, And its pinions with glistening gold." (Psalm 68:13)*

Heaven is filled with gold and precious stone dust, Glenn Smith describes what he saw in heaven,

> *"One of the things I had seen was the fact that the dirt of heaven is made of diamonds, sapphires, and many jewels."*[71]

---

[71] Smith, p.44

Stones Start Appearing All Around the World

Gateway Christian Fellowship in Coeur D'Alene, Idaho had been praying for years to see God's glory manifest. In the early 2000s they had a Glory Explosion conference with Jeff Jansen, Joshua Mills, and David Herzog where gold crowns appeared in people's mouths, gold dust appeared on peoples clothing and skin, and people lost weight instantly. Some had open visions and many people were healed. The church began to pray for the gemstones' manifestation and for God's glory to appear. On June 8th of 2006, their prayers were answered and forty big stones appeared over a few weeks.

These stones were eventually taken to a series of jewellers to determine authenticity. One professional noted that the gemstones lacked flaws, which is impossible on earth, as all naturally occurring stones have inclusions. Possibly even more interesting is the fact that they lacked the inclusions found in man-made stones as well.[72]

> "In Carolina, Puerto Rico, just outside of San Juan, there used to be a church called Casa De Restoration de Misericordia (House of Restoration and Mercy). The senior Pastor, Pastor Denis Rojas, began pastoring the church in 2003 after he and his wife Pastor Awilda had spent 25 years as evangelists. On April 22nd of 2004 they obtained a building and gave it its name. The Lord had indicated to them that they should find a house where they could live in and perform miracles, and that God's

---

[72] King, p. 105

name would be glorified in many places as a result of the manifestations that He would bring through them."[73]

Pastor Denis was in that building for two years with oil manifestations and gold dust appearing. Also, sapphire-coloured dust began to appear, ruby dust, emerald dust and silver dust started to appear over many months in church meetings. As the church grew in membership, they transferred to another building. The first gemstone appeared on a Monday during prayer and intercession, months after the myrrh oil had started to flow. The first gemstone to fall was a square diamond that hit Pastor Awilda on the back. As she held the stone she saw the stone changing colours with light.

As Michael King says,

"This was a watershed event for the church because after that gemstones began to appear - one, two, five, twenty, and more! The pastors noted that the quantity of the stones appeared to be linked to the level of adoration of God present in the church at the time. At those times, often angels would leave diamonds behind, which they believed represented how the Lord feels about the church. As of September 22nd, 2007, the church had 1285 gems appear, but by November they had at least 1885 gems that they documented in a register. When the Bible was left open on the podium, its pages would always be found turned to the last page of Psalms and first page of Proverbs. This manifestation of oil, gold dust, and gemstones from heaven lasted for over four years."[74]

Linda Cruz in her book, *All His Jewels; From Glory to Glory*, writes,

---

[73] King, p 107
[74] King p. 110

"Labour Day weekend of **2006**, I attended a conference in Nashville, Tennessee, where I interviewed several attendees about this new phenomenon. At least two people related personal stories to me of jewels manifesting. The leader of the conference, Jeff Jansen, showed me a ruby that supernaturally appeared in one of his meetings. As he held it in the palm of his hand, I observed its dark red colour and faceted face."[75]

Mary Task in her book, *The 12 Gemstones of Revelation; Unlocking The Significance of the Gemstones Phenomenon*, writes,

"Things began changing for Pastor Len and his congregation. It all started with eight weeks of special meetings held at his church. That's when feathers began randomly falling during their services amidst healings, miracles, and a number of salvations. And then there was the gold dust. Who could explain that? However, the thing that seemed to top it all began in late 2007 when perfect little gemstones began falling throughout the church sanctuary. 'We could hear the gemstones hitting the chairs and then bouncing to the floor,' Pastor Len explained.
Some of the gemstones were diamonds and some were amethyst stones; all were about half the size of a fingernail. One of the amethyst stones was taken to a jeweller who confirmed its authenticity and estimated its value at around $30."[76]
"In Washington, Leola reported that the small collection of gemstones she had found in her home, and at several different services through **2008**, appeared to be increasing in size. And, also, at a small church in Colville Washington, it was reported that, even as the preacher stood in front of the sanctuary, several eyewitnesses saw gemstones appearing mid-air before dropping to the floor. An estimated 200 gemstones, some of which were amethysts, were collected in a single morning."[77]

---

[75] Linda Cruz, All His Jewels, Xulon Press, 2007, p. 4
[76] Mary Trask, The 12 Gemstones of Revelation; Unlocking The Significance of the Gemstones Phenomenon, *Destiny Image, 2009,* 2009, p. 59
[77] Trask, p. 150

"In Redding, California, young David and his wife Taylor had just returned from a prayer meeting where small, perfectly cut diamonds had been found in the carpet of the home where they and others had gathered to pray. Later that night, as they prepared for bed, they pulled back the covers to find a large, heart-shaped diamond resting atop the middle of their mattress. Curious, they brought the large diamond to a gemmologist for examination. After studying the flawless stone, he promptly offered them $10,000 for the diamond."[78]

A Testimony from Len Lacroix in Hungary,

Crystal Gems from Heaven,
"On March 19, 2012, during our family prayer meeting, we experienced an open heaven over us and I felt the presence of the Lord. After our Morning Prayer and breakfast, Jennifer discovered a supernatural gem in our bedroom. She said, "I was thinking about going to heaven and people that I want to see. I thought that I just want to get rid of everything – all the worthless things of this earth – and leave it all behind for the Lord's sake. So I was cleaning out the shelf in our bedroom closet, and I got to where my basket was. I moved my basket and there was a little, crystal-like gem. I immediately thought it was a supernatural gem from heaven. As I looked more closely at how it was shaped and it seemed to have a perfect cut with many facets. Then I walked into the kitchen thinking that this is really from the Lord."

As I was sitting at the table, finishing my breakfast, she walked in and said to me, "Look what I found in my closet! I think it may be a jewel from heaven!" And she handed it to me. As she placed the gem in my hand, I felt the presence of the Lord all over me. I said, "Jennifer, I can feel the presence of the Lord all over me right now! The Lord gave you this to show you how much He loves you!"

A little while later, she was back in our bedroom again, drying her hair, and looked over at another shelf in the closet. She wondered whether she might find something else in there. Then

---

[78] Trask, p 15

she turned away from the closet, and pondered how the Lord has been giving supernatural gems to His people in the US, Africa, and other places. She wondered if He was going to do the same thing here in this spiritual wasteland, because the glory of God needs to come. She said, "As I once again turned back toward the closet, there on the floor lay another crystal-like gem. It was laying perfectly face up in the carpet."

I was in my office when Jennifer came in and shouted, "Len! Look!" And she showed me in her hand a gem just like the first one, which was larger, but had the exact same cut! We went into the bedroom, and she showed me where she found it. <u>It had been on the floor, in the exact center of the spot where the glory of God appeared two nights ago.</u> Then we were certain it was from the Lord. As we looked at it in the light under a magnifying glass, it had a perfect cut with many facets. When we put the smaller one beside it, we could see that they were both cut exactly alike. As I held them in the palm of my hand and looked through the magnifying glass, <u>I could see the details of my palm print perfectly and clearly through the stone</u>.

I said, "Jennifer, I felt the presence of the Lord when you placed the first one in my hand earlier. I know this is from the Lord." Then we all knelt down and praised the Lord profusely, not for anything he could give us, but for Who He is. We declared that He is more beautiful than diamonds, more precious than silver, more costly than gold, and nothing that we desire compared with Him.

She said that as she was praying yesterday, she heard the Lord say, "It is my Father's good pleasure to give you the kingdom." Last night as she was going off to bed, she thought that she would need to use our electronic Bible to find that passage. She opened the Bible and read a passage. At the end of the passage, she read, "But seek His kingdom, and these things will be added to you. Do not be afraid, little flock, for your Father has chosen gladly to give you the kingdom." (Luk 12:31-32). She said, "Wow! That's the verse!" And she hadn't even gone searching for it. She wasn't actively looking for it. So that confirmed it had been the Lord speaking this to her. So when these gems appeared this morning, it further confirmed that the Father has chosen to give us the kingdom.

When she tried placing the gem back into the carpet in the same position it was in when she found it, she could not get it to sit perfectly upright like it had been when she found it. She commented later, "It's the latter rain! It's raining!" We also tried dropping it from eye level onto the carpet and it always bounced away. Later in the afternoon, I spoke by phone with my Christian cousin, back in the States, who is a certified gemologist. I told him about these and he said that if I place the stones face down on a printed page, such as a magazine, and can read the text, then they are not diamonds. He said that when it is a diamond, you couldn't read the text through the stone. He asked me to take a photo and send it to him. So rather than use just any text, I decided to use God's Word, in order to take a photo of the stones face-down on some text. I opened Jennifer's Bible to Proverbs 8, where it was book marked, and I placed the stones right on the verse that says, "Take my instruction and not silver, And knowledge rather than choicest gold. For wisdom is better than jewels; And all desirable things cannot compare with her." (Prov. 8:10-11). We were unable to read the text through the stones. It was distorted. I took the photos and some video footage of it to send to my cousin. He wrote back saying his first impression is that these are glass jewels. This testimony is part of something much greater that God has been doing in our lives here in Hungary since January 1, 2012".[79]

From Kathie Walters, 2016,

"Around three or four years ago gemstones began to appear in our house. We don't know where they came from or what they were about. We had heard that other Christians had experienced the same phenomena. The gemstones came in different sizes, so we put them in a box. When we looked at them several days later, two different ones had multiplied and now we had two different sets with identical gemstones. Some of those gemstones also

---

[79] http://budapesttestimonies.blogspot.com/2012/04/gems-from-heaven.html

increased in size. The last time this kind of thing happened was about two years ago."[80]

---

[80] https://kathiewaltersministry.com/2016/05/15/god-miracles-or-atheism/

MY FIRST EXPOSURE!

My first exposure to the Gemstone manifesting reality, started when I went to visit a friend who ran an Orphanage in the jungles of India. They had just been through great persecution, and the Lord had started to visit them in a very powerful way. The Holy Spirit came in incredible power and presence, and the children in worship would be taken over by the Holy Spirit and caught up into trances (Acts 10:10) and visions of heaven (Acts 7:55). When the Holy Spirit came upon them, they would go into visions and fall on the floor as if they were asleep. When they woke up, they would get up and retell the wonders they had seen in Heaven with Jesus. Now, one may say: "STOP RIGHT THERE, this is just hallucinations, this proves nothing!"

BUT, what does one say, when a child is on the floor in a vision, (I'm sitting next to them, and their hand is open and empty), and as they awaken, you see their hand close tightly shut; then as they stand to their feet and declare that "Jesus gave them a gemstone in Heaven," and on opening their hand, the stone is sparkling on their palm? It is a little harder to deny. This I saw many times... I saw it in India and in New Zealand. I've even seen children come out of visions, open their mouths and gemstones fall out. I've also been in houses and seen them appear before my eyes all through the house.

Psalms 81:10 says,

> *"I am the Lord your God, who brought you out of the land of Egypt: open your mouth wide, and I will fill it."*

In his book, *The Treasury of David*, Charles Spurgeon indicates that "an ancient custom of Persian Kings was to invite honoured guests to open wide their mouths, so the King could cram them with sweetmeats. If he was particularly pleased with an individual, jewels would sometimes be included in the mouthful.[81]

I have seen it so many times now, that I know there is no magic, deceit or falseness about this phenomenon.

I was once in New Zealand, standing in a park, and I felt the Holy Spirit come upon me. As I turned around, I saw a man sitting on a bench. I felt led to go over to him and share some of my experiences. Just as I was about to leave, I looked down on the ground and by his foot was a gemstone, which had manifested. I picked it up and gave it to him as confirmation of what I had just been sharing.

I can remember going to Germany with a few of my stones on me. These were glassy ones, and at this large conference, I pulled them out to show two Pastors. The stones in my hand came alive, pulsating with presence. As one of the Pastors put his hand over my hand, he was slain on the floor by the presence of God on the stones. They are real, not fake – don't be too quick to rubbish the simple things or those things that can confound the wise.

I have also experienced the supernatural appearance of money. I was on my weekly 10 km walk going up and down the streets of local houses. I was longing to buy myself a treat. I was hard up, and it had been months since I had brought myself something to enjoy (the little things). I was short of $10 in getting my treat and I had counted all my spare coins.

---

[81] Mary Trask, *The 12 Gemstones of Revelation: Unlocking The Significance of the Gemstones Phenomenon*, Destiny Image, 2009, p.18

While walking I got caught up in my thoughts and my surroundings kind of faded. In my mind I could see myself preaching a faith sermon, building up faith, that money could appear. After a few minutes I realised that I was caught up in my thoughts and needed to concentrate on the road. As the surroundings came back into my full attention, I looked down at my feet and there was a $10 note just in front of my shoes on the pavement. I believe it supernaturally appeared.

I have heard over the years that Charlie Shamp, from Destiny Encounters, has received gemstones in his meetings; Rob Deluca has received gemstones manifesting in his Church; Ian Clayton of Sons of Thunder Ministries has had a gemstone manifest/come out of his hand, Justin Paul Abraham's from Company of Burning Hearts Ministries, has had them manifest and appear in his house. Now, this occurrence is not just happening around the lives of top Christian Leaders, it's also happening to simple, genuine, unknown Believers all around the world. I've even heard of a guy who received some gemstones and sold them for $6000 to buy a van to go around and preach the Gospel.

I have seen documentation from a guy called Jason Cuellar, who wanted to silence sceptics about his gemstones, showing a report from a Gemmologist, who confirmed all were real stones and had a price value of $3500. Jeff Jansen has had stones appear in meetings, that have been tested, and are cut so perfect they are believed to not be of this world (50 Carat Rubies).

Jason Cobb, and his children in India have experienced many stones manifesting and being brought down while in heaven visions,

"On the 21st of October, 2009, following persecution, focused prayer and heightened praise, the Holy Spirit visited our community in an extraordinary way. The spiritual eyes of the believing children in our Children's Home were miraculously opened, and they were caught up into Heaven, an experience that has continued on a near-daily basis, since then. From the early days, the children tried to bring back from their visits to Heaven, many kinds of Heavenly treasures, including Heavenly stones. We saw many looks of bewilderment on the faces of returning children, as the stones that were so real in the spiritual Kingdom were now not present in this natural world. We prompted them to ask Jesus about this. In Heaven, Jesus told a group of visiting children, 'Keep praying, one day they will come through.' It took two years of focused prayer before the breakthrough came.

"One night, when we were having our regular Heaven prayer, our daughter walked up to my wife and I with her eyes closed, while in a Heavenly trance. She said, 'Mum, this is from Jesus.' She then opened her hand and in it was a beautifully faceted stone, resembling a diamond. She then closed her hand and came over to me and said, 'Dad, this is from Jesus.' She then opened her hand again, and there was a second stone of the same shape and size. When she returned from her Heavenly experience, she confirmed that Jesus had personally given her two stones to deliver to my wife and I. She was overwhelmed with joy to learn that the stones had actually come through after many months of trying. Before our very eyes, we witnessed an amazing miracle, the spiritual substance had become a physical substance. Following this initial manifestation, our community has had the joy of seeing many hundreds of stones transition from Heaven to earth."[82]

---

[82] In personal correspondence .

Encounters from others,

Ben Lewis:

"After Richy came back from India and told me about gemstones, I was fascinated, so I started to declare and pray for them to manifest in my house. About a year later, I found my first one and was blown away. The second one I found, appeared in our prayer room. it literally was not there one minute and then the next, I saw it shining and picked it up. I have found three so far. For me, it's a sign from God saying, 'I can do anything, do you believe?'"

Judy Abrahams:

"A couple of years ago when Jason and Jo visited my house, some of the grandkids came, and gems started showing up on the stairs and in the kid's room upstairs; small clear ones and coloured ones. We called friends with kids and gave each one a small plastic bag, and they all found about ten each. We called more friends and more got found. One granddaughter said, 'Nanny I want a purple one.' I said, 'Ask Jesus.' She did, and a few minutes later, she came to me saying she had found two purple ones. One of my friends had been earlier in the day saying she wanted a purple one. So, I told my Danika, 'You need to give one of your purple ones to Penny,' who was her neighbour. So, she did. Jo said that altogether that day, 280 gems came through into my house. God is so cool."

Sjaan Rounds:

"Ruby just found another gem at school the other day in the toilets. This is her third, I think, that she has found at school. But when we were putting it away with the others, we noticed our little blue one, that Pat found by my feet had changed to a light green colour! So amazing! It wasn't long after, I read about yours changing colour."

Fiona Dieleman:

"It had been a rather challenging morning at church, and I had been doubting my own discernment and feeling a little bit discouraged. That evening, I was the first person into the prayer room for the prayer meeting and was arranging some chairs, when a small sparkle against the wall caught my eye. It was a reasonably big purple/pink gemstone, not the full-on sparkly kind, but I knew it was from the Lord, nonetheless, letting me know that He was in the midst of my day and my discouragement."

Stones Manifest Throughout NZ

After the stones started to manifest at the Orphanage, it wasn't long after that a couple from the Orphanage visited New Zealand from India and the stones started to manifest all throughout the country as they mingled. The stones have continued to appear for a number of years at different people's places since.

Angela Curtis has documented this with wonderful testimonies in her second heaven book, *Explore With Me in Paradise*, and gives useful dates!

> *In 2014 - "Mericia Hall - I first encountered the miracle of gems appearing when Jan, Jase, and his two daughters Chris and Jess visited New Zealand in 2014. It was an extraordinary time, as it seemed wherever they went, gems would appear. We found them under our feet, on table, bench tops, all over the floor, on beds, and down stairways. On one occasion, I placed a little plastic bag on a dresser and returned a few minutes later to find a large white gem inside the bag. It was exhilarating to be present in this tremendous outpouring of God's signs and wonders. These precious gems were in the most glorious colours, shapes and sizes. Some were double pointed, with gold or silver on one side. But the best part was the joy and laughter that accompanied their appearance."[83]*

> *In 2015 - "Maggie Carrasquillo - We've travelled extensively around the world over the years, and have had some pretty amazing experiences. God has frequently shown up and we love it. However, in 2015, in the beautiful country of New Zealand, our paradigms were shattered. We were invited to visit a sister at her house so we could meet a beautiful woman from India named Jan. We sat around the table and spoke about Heaven for hours. Her testimonies were incredible and beyond anything we*

---

[83] Curtis, p.113

had ever heard before. Then I noticed my husband staring at the floor with a look of awe on his face. He pointed to numerous places all around the room. There were gems appearing all over the floor. We watched them materialise right in front of us. Where there was nothing before, one would appear. We immediately jumped out of our seats and collected them. They were all the same colour and the same size, and they were perfect. I've never seen or experienced anything like it. I was a little freaked out because they just kept appearing and it didn't stop. I excused myself and went to the bathroom to give myself a moment to process what was happening. I needed to wrap my mind around not just what I had witnessed and was still happening in the next room. There was no way I could deny it because I'd held the stones in my hands. I was questioning in my mind how this could be possible when right there in the restroom more gems appeared everywhere.[84]"

In May 2019 - "Bev Oliver - At the launch of "Talk With Me In Paradise" (book launch), the miracle occurred again. Before the speeches began, Heaven joined earth. Suddenly, stones appeared all over the hall floor. I giggled, suggesting we should have called the event the 'Bottom's Up Club'. Both children and grownups were down on their hands and knees, finding gems just released from Heaven above. Hundreds of beautifully cut stones were liberally sent to be a blessing and prove the miraculous events written about in the book. No one could refute the truth. Our God proves His love for us time and again with the appearance of His kingdom jewels."[85]

And there are even more recent manifestations,

2023 - Jeremy Morgan from New Zealand - A YWAM brother has had round stones manifest.

---

[84] Curtis, p. 112
[85] Curtis, p.120

2023 - Stephen Powell from United States Arizona - A diamond manifested right near the pulpit as he was ministering on "healing the broken heart".

Conclusions - Recent history shows us that the stones have been manifesting for many years in different places and times and seasons. I can only report on the accounts that I have found in my research, there are most likely many more occurrences, but it seems like there are seasons where the stones come and go for some time also. Sometimes the stones stop manifesting because people's intimacy with God is not as strong and motives of the heart have changed or it can just be that God's season for the stones have ended.

From My Research We Can Form Some Important Historical Dates

1447 - St. Colette - Stone in crucifix from heaven.
1948 - Golden Candle-Stick ladies - Raptured in jewels and clothing.
1980 - Glenn Smith - Prophecy of a new season of stones coming.
2000 - Ruth Ward Heflin - Prophesied about the gemstones coming.
2000 - Gateway Christian Fellowship - Glory conference prayed for the stones.
2004 - In Carolina, Puerto Rico - Gold, sapphire dust and gemstones manifest.
2006 - Gateway Christian Fellowship - The stones started to manifest.
2007 - Pastor Len and his congregation - Little gemstones began falling throughout the church.
2008 - Church in Colville Washington - 200 gemstones manifest.
2009 - Jason Cobb - Children in heavenly visions tried to bring stones back from heaven.
2011 - Orphanage Children after two years of prayer - The stones manifest on earth in their campus.
2012 - Len Lacroix in Hungary.
2014 - Mericia Hall - Gemstones manifest throughout the house
2015 - Maggie Carrasquillo - Gemstones manifest throughout the house.
2016 - Kathie Walters.
2019 - Book launch of, "Talk With Me In Paradise" - Stones manifest all over the floor.

2023 - Stephen Powell - Diamonds manifest on his bible preaching.

2024 - Senior Pastor Othusite Mmusi and founder at Glory Invasion International Church has witnessed many gemstones manifest.

Intermediate Realm

The intermediate realm is the crossing over realm. When a person dies, they leave their body and believers go through a portal of light into the dimensions of heaven.

> *"Have the gates of death been revealed to you? Or have you seen the doors of the shadow of death? Have you comprehended the breadth of the earth? Tell Me, if you know all this. "Where is the way to the dwelling of light, And darkness, where is its place" (Job 38:17-19)*

Many near death experiences encounter this tunnel of bright light.

A friend of mine was high up in a tree cutting branches off as one big branch broke off and hit him in his face knocking him out of the tree. He fell a long way down smashing his body and head on to the floor. Family members ran out to see him and found him dead without a pulse. They began sobbing with tears and fright and started praying with all their hearts strength. After at least thirty minutes my friend gasped for breath and came back into his body. He was rushed to hospital and had a number of broken bones, but what was amazing, apart from coming back from the dead was what he saw on the other side. He had, had a near death experience. It was a near death experience because he came back, but he was in fact dead in the physical.

He describes going through bright light and standing in a place where there were stone blocks engraved. These were precious, coloured stones in a wall.

He recalls,

> *"Yes, I did see words engraved into each stone block. The engraved words were highlighted in black. The letters were a very beautiful olden styled font like Old English style. The words were written in another language so I could not read them but I had a strong knowing that these stones & words were records of different aspects of my life. It did look / feel like a temple."*

What was this place? to be honest as a Theologian I am not sure. I am going to be careful what I say here and give ideas of what this place could be and not dictate the experience. It seems to be a record, timeline, deposit of one's life and works in stone. Scripture does talk about the apostles having their names written in the foundation stones in heaven, so there is a causal link of writing on heavenly stones.

> *"The city was built on twelve foundation stones. On each of the stones was **written** the **name** of one of the Lamb's twelve **apostles"** (Revelation 21:14)*

But I believe a better link is,

> *"Therefore, you are no longer strangers and foreigners, but fellow citizens with the saints and members of God's household,* **built on the foundation of the apostles and prophets, with Christ Jesus Himself as the cornerstone.** *In Him the whole building is fitted together and grows into a holy temple in the Lord." (Ephesians 2:20)*

If the apostles and prophets have names written into foundation stones, then we know they are real stones and we are told, "You" too, are built upon the foundation laid by the **apostles**

and prophets, the **cornerstone** being **Christ Jesus** himself. We are written into the walls of the Temple.

> *"To them I will give in My Temple and within My walls a memorial, And a name better than that of sons and daughters; I will give them an everlasting name which will not be eliminated." (Isaiah 56:5)*

The word "Memorial" means - A ceremony to remember someone who has died, serving to preserve remembrance. A structure established to remind people of a person or event. Within the walls, that is a section of the wall, it holds a record of a person's life.

> *"Can a woman forget her nursing child, or lack compassion for the son of her womb? Even if she could forget, I will not forget you! Behold, I have inscribed you on the palms of My hands; your walls are ever before Me." (Isaiah 49:16)*

Behold I have inscribed you, your walls are ever before me. These walls, are precious stones with witting on them. The stones will speak and echo one's life.

> *"For the stones will cry out from the wall, and the beams from the timbers will echo it." (Habakkuk 2:11)*

> *"O you afflicted one, Tossed with tempest, and not comforted, Behold, I will lay your stones with colorful gems, And lay your foundations with sapphires." (Isaiah 54:11)*

Our lives are built upon Jesus and the apostles and prophets foundations stones of the temple. Our works, the record of our days and motives will be inscribed in precious stones for all to see as one's work will become clear, for the day will declare it.

> *"Now if anyone builds on this foundation with gold, silver, precious stones, each one's work will become clear, for the day will declare it."*
> *(1 Corinthians 3:12-15)*
>
> *"The one who is victorious I will make a pillar in the temple of my God. Never again will they leave it." (Revelation 3:12)*

The Temple was also a treasury room which held the wealth of people's talents and life's work. Could these Scriptures give insights to my friend's experience?

In Heaven - Crossed Over!

Those who do die and cross over the veil into heaven also have the ability to interact with gemstones and send them down as gifts for others on the earth. This may sound far-fetched, but is true as the story below will document. The idea that those who have passed away can interact with others on earth is clearly seen in the biblical example of Moses and Elijah on the mountain of transfiguration.

Several years ago, at the children's home in India where the children were experiencing daily heaven encounters. A young girl there had a severe mental disability; she needed almost everything done for her. But one day the Lord came for her and took her life. That night in the children's encounters with heaven they saw her there, her body transformed like a beautiful princess. As the children came out of their visions on the campus prayer room floor, gemstones exploded out of the atmosphere in the room and covered the floor. It was a gift from her from heaven.

A lady who had visited the children's home many times[86] who spent much time caring for this young girl with love, on one visit after her passing was given a beautiful green stone brought down by one of the children in their heaven encounter with the girl, a gift given for all the precious love and care she had shown her on earth.

---

[86] Judy Abrahams.

Looking Around Heaven

> *"But you have come to Mount Zion, to the city of the living God, the heavenly Jerusalem. You have come to thousands upon thousands of angels in joyful assembly." (Hebrews 12:22)*

In the Book of Enoch, it describes God's house of fire the inner heart of God,

> *"And I beheld a vision... there was a second house, greater than the former... and it was built of flames of fire, and its floor was of fire, and above it were lightnings and the path of the stars, and its ceiling also was flaming fire. And I looked and saw therein a lofty throne; its appearance was as crystal and the wheels thereof as the shining sun, and there was the vision of cherubim. And from underneath the throne came streams of flaming fire so that I could not look thereon. And the Great Glory sat thereon, and His raiment shone more brightly than the sun...the flaming fire was around about Him and a great fire stood before Him." (1 Enoch 14:15-22)*

The Book of Enoch goes on to reveal about the precious stones of fire, which in them held the secrets of God. Enoch talks of being shown in a vision the secrets of righteousness and mercy; these were part of the precious stones in God's heart. They contained the mysteries of God,

> *"Afterwards my spirit was concealed, ascending into the Heavens. I beheld the sons of the holy angels treading on flaming fire, whose garments and robes were white, and whose countenances were transparent as crystal. I saw two rivers of fire glittering like the hyacinth. Then I fell on my face before the Lord of Spirits. And Michael, one of the*

archangels, took me by the right hand, raised me up, and brought me out to where was every secret of mercy and secret of righteousness. He showed me all the hidden things of the extremities of Heaven, all the receptacles of the stars, and the splendours of all, from whence they went forth before the face of the holy. And he concealed the spirit of Enoch in the Heaven of Heavens. There I beheld, in the midst of that light, a building raised with stones of ice. And in the midst of the stones, vibrations of living fire. My spirit saw around the circle of this flaming habitation, on one of its extremities, that there was a river full of living fire which encompassed it." (Enoch 70: 1-8) (emphasis mine).

Where Enoch talks of stones of ice, this is a reference to looking like crystal, like burning white light, and in the midst of this habitation were stones absorbing the frequency of the vibrating flames of fire imprinting the secrets of God into the precious stones of fire. Precious stones hold frequencies, energies, and vibrations of coded mysteries.

We have seen throughout this book, that wherever stones show up, they are representing us nearby. It is here in the heart of God, where we came from and first lived.

For Enoch goes on to say,

"Then that angel came to me, and with his voice saluted me, saying 'they are the offspring of man who are born for righteousness'." (1 Enoch 14:17)

We are created in God's image, perfect before we come to earth. As living stones, the stones of fire reflect God's nature, and they speak of us. Lucifer covered the stones of fire to be like God in character, but he also covered us as living spirits in God's heart, for he was our guardian over us.

Ian Clayton's experience in heaven,

"The river flows out from where the veil sits, at the edge of the Throne. Because of Who and what God is, He continues to create all the time. The mountain is forever growing because of Who He is. He is forever creating, it just grows! Shaking and earthquakes often happen, and so diamonds fall of the mountain. So, there is a cascade of diamonds coming off the mountain and the oil of the presence of God flowing off the mountain, so you get diamonds and oil mixed together. The Bible talks about the River being as clear as crystal. It is as clear as crystal because there is crystal in it. But you cannot see the crystals until you jump in! There are jewels in the River... As I sank in, I was breathing pure diamonds and oil into my nose, my mouth and my body. I stayed there for about half an hour thinking, "Lord, I am identifying with you, I am identifying with Who You are, in baptism of the River of Glory..." I was finding that I was changing on the inside without having to do anything. I was beginning to immerse myself in the very nature of the One who made me. I have taught about the skin of God. The reason there are diamonds and oil that flow as part of the River is because God is Who He is. What sheds off Him is residue and the residue makes a river. It cannot be controlled; it just flows out under the curtain and then it becomes a raging torrent of His glory to the earth.
When I came out of the River, just like honey sticks to your arm, my skin was covered with oil and diamonds and my skin looked like the skin of God. I was covered with oil and little diamonds all over my body."[87]

Another witness,

"Flowing out from under His throne of light is an amazing river called the River of Life. This river is God's life-giving presence, not just in Heaven, but for all His creation on earth as well. The river itself is breath-taking. It flows out and separates into four rivers that flow in different directions throughout Heaven. In

---

[87] Ian Clayton, p. 119-121

some areas the water is as clear as crystal. So much so that you can see reflections coming off the bottom as it flows from the throne of the Father and Jesus the King. In other areas of Heaven, the river contains amazing colours that swirl randomly as if they too are worshipping God with their creativity. The unique beauty of the colours and clarity of the water are not seen in rivers anywhere else. Based on where the river is located, the colours are different. Some represent the different nations, gifts, fruits, mantels, commissions, blessings, also spiritual maturity and accessibility. It flows throughout the kingdom, displaying revelations of God Himself."[88]

The river is God's presence and when you are in the river or drinking from the river you are being transformed into His likeness. I find it interesting that different locations, most likely the closer to the throne you are represent spiritual maturity and accessibility. This reveals that it matters how you live on earth and one's transformation in sanctification will open locations to them that others will not have.

One of the first real heaven encounter books to be written is called, '40 Days in Heaven: The True Testimony of Seneca Sodi's Visitation to Paradise, the Holy City and the Glory of God's Throne', (1909 AD). Seneca tells us,

"The Light toward the City which I had seen on my first arrival grew more and more glorious as we neared the City. We could at length see the shining of the jasper wall. You see that great Judean gate over there? Its frame and hinges are of the purest gold and set with one great pearl. This gate always stands open, for there is no restraint in heaven. Unbound liberty is now yours forever. And the wall has respect to those outside as well as to those inside. The angel at the gateway is to give direction to all who may inquire. You will further remember that there are twelve of these gates as well as twelve foundations, and there are twelve angels as well as twelve gates. No one can enter these

---

[88] Curtis, p. 134

gates not fully prepared. Did you notice some who dropped back far into the rear? In the world, the truth had to be observed for any advancement. This wall with its gates, marks definite experience in the journey of the redeemed. It is a fuller development of the great truths suggested by the ancient tabernacle; the holy and the most holy place has reference to the saints on earth and those in heaven. Surely, said the elder, when you are prepared for the light and glory of the city, you will be brought to its gates and ushered in with the welcome of your Lord. If you wait among the trees, do not be restless nor neglectful. Almost the entire catalogue of the Christian graces must be learned by you (on earth, or in heaven – outside the city). Partake freely of the twelve kinds of fruit on the trees, they will impart light, life and grace to your soul. Press the leaves to your nostrils and bind them to your heart and no taint of evil will remain in you."[89]

Inside the Gates of Heaven by Oden Hetrick, another heaven encounter book, says,

> *"So also, as we approach God's abode in the sky, we come first to the large Outer Court or suburbs, then to the Holy Place, then to the Most Holy Place where God sits on His Throne. Now, these suburbs of the City of Heaven are very much like earth, with grass, flowers, trees, shadows, birds and animals. This is the place where spiritual principles must be learned by those saints who on earth did not become very spiritually-minded. It is not true that we suddenly know everything when we get to Heaven. Christians on earth are admonished by Scripture. Study to show yourself approved of God. — 2 Timothy 2:15."*[90]

Everything that is created has a token, a representation, yoked in a precious stone. That being, whatever reflects God's nature and character, which is seen in His son's or daughter's "hearts"

---

[89] Elwood Scott, 40 Days in Heaven, First Fruits Offering, 2008, p. 36
[90] Oden Hetrick, Inside the Gates of Heaven, Advanced Global Publishing, 20014.

and achievements and transformations (for where your heart is your treasure shall be[91]). There are stones that reflect God's spiritual atmosphere of creation, life, growth, peace, beauty, glory, righteousness, health, and Kingdom ownership.

Every coloured stone has a different meaning and purpose, and they reflect the rainbow river of God. These stones that are produced in the river from our works can flow to earth and bring about a spiritual healing effect upon creation[92].

A Child's testimony out of a heaven encounter,

"Jesus walked with me to the Rainbow River, and we met King Solomon there. He gave me a blue gem and told me to throw it into the blue part of the Rainbow River. So, I did. I get lots of different coloured stones from King Solomon. He tells me to put them in the part of the river that matches the stones. 'What do the stones mean?' I asked King Solomon one day. 'Every stone has a meaning behind it,' he said. 'Each one will have a positive influence over the campus. I'll tell you the meaning of the colours each time I give you one. Today's stone is blue, which means it will bring more water and rain to the campus.' The next day, I met King Solomon again. He gave me a green coloured stone. 'Put it in the green part of the river,' he said, 'Green is for growth for the flowers and trees on the campus."[93]

---

[91] Matthew 6:21

[92] As was mention in the "Introduction" about Ezekiel/Revelation's heavenly temple river - healing everything it touches.

[93] Curtis, Book 1 - p.73

Atmosphere of Praise!
Loss and Gains

For heaven to come to earth, for the things of heaven to materialise on earth there must be great praise on earth. God encamps His presence in our praises. For the stones to manifest on earth heavens portals must open and the veil be saturated with praise and worship. Without praise the stones will not come through. They may come down behind the veil, but without the praise they will be lost. Prayer can move the angels to bring the stones down behind the veil on plates or in their wings and feathers, but it is the atmosphere of "praise residue" that opens the door for them to materialise.

In heaven around the throne God's presence flows, and there is twenty-four-hour praise and worship from the angels and saints, singing holy, holy, holy is the Lord God Almighty. It is no wonder that the stones are created out of God and flow down into the river and are given out to the angels to deliver. There is an atmosphere of awe and wonder of high praise, this is what must be reproduced and displayed on the earth.

I don't think it needs to be twenty-four hours a day, but the greater the amount the stronger the presence of God will be and the wider the portals will open on earth.

Treasure Rooms and Lost Property!

In heaven there are buildings and walls that hold our treasure that we have attained, earned, and have shown ourselves approved, and there are even rooms with lost property.

Seneca Sodi explains,

"Bohemond and I now walked a short distance to a most remarkable cluster of buildings which Moses had just pointed out to me. They were massive, stupendous, and grand. They occupied one whole block of the city and seemed to be foursquare. A great inscription was written above the threshold, 'Treasure laid Up in heaven.'
"We spent a long time going from place to place looking into these wonderful treasures, which God's people have secured for themselves, as well as rejected blessings which might have been secured by diligent effort while on earth, for we found that all these multitudes of holy gems, jewels, pearls and lovely garments all had their counterpart in the experience of saints on earth. These heavenly jewels might have been easily secured and would have added much to the riches of the soul in the heavenly kingdom."

Scripture does warn us that we can lose property by the way we live on earth, *'Watch out that you do not lose what we have worked for, but that you may be rewarded fully." 2 John 1:8)*. But let us press on and store our treasure in heaven for where your heart is your treasure will be. I find it amazing that others have also seen these rooms and walls of treasures. We must remember that Seneca Sodi's account was from the 1900s.

Jan Rainbow, living in the present has seen these places in her heaven encounters[94]. She recalls a wall in heaven holding all the

---

[94] Jan Rainbow had no knowledge of these other accounts, she saw first hand.

stones that people had rejected on earth or lost due to wrong motives of the heart,

> *"It made me sad they stopped looking to the One who created it. Instead, they took His gift for granted. The Lord knowing this, showed me a wall in Heaven. It was where all the stones were placed when they were given but not treasured, or used for the purpose each stone carried. I rejoiced that day, knowing that none were lost or forsaken."*[95]

How amazing the Lord creates treasure to record our transforming glory and releases these stone with anointings to empower our walks on earth and status in heaven. And how amazing is it that when God creates a blessing it cannot be forgotten, even if rejected, but is stored in heavens walls.

> *"If we are faithless, He remains faithful; He cannot deny Himself." (2 Timothy 2:13)*

---

[95] Curtis, book 2 - p. 100

Jesus the Master Carpenter/Jeweller

We are told in Scripture that if we are faithful throughout our lives, we will receive the Crown of Life. This doesn't mean we will be excluded if we make a mistake or endure trials, but we are told that there is a 'Crown of Life' for those who keep running the race faithfully.

> *"Be faithful until death, and I will give you the crown of life." (Revelation 2:10)*

On reading this verse, we must go another layer deeper. Not only do we receive a crown, it is a crown about our life; and it's alive and moving. Testimony has revealed that this Crown grows throughout our lives, and Jesus adds to it as we accomplish victories and assignments. This Crown is a crown of our life's history on earth, and it is living, moving and interacting with our heartbeat. In the Crown are tokens, symbols, precious stones, and heavenly objects that tell the testimony of our lives. In Heaven, our crown will appear on our heads as we come to the throne. In worship, many lay their crowns down before the Throne, and those crowns will dance/speak forth, move in front of Him, and tell the stories of our lives, of what we have overcome by God's Grace for His Glory.

> *"They lay their crowns before the throne"*
> *(Revelation 4:9-10)*

The crown the believer obtains, is the victor's crown (Greek - stephanos). Historically, a perishable wreath was given for victory in the games, achievements in war, and places of honour.

In contrast, the crown the believer obtains from God is eternal and comes from faithfulness, and as one can lose other crowns, this one is the story of our life that we will place before the King each time we come to the Throne, manifesting in a living 'art form' His glory in us. So, we must walk carefully...

There are other crowns that can be merited, the crown of glory for special recognition for Shepherding the flock (1 Peter 5:1-4), and the crown of righteousness for upright behaviour, a righteous life lived (2 Timothy 4:6-8).

Jewish tradition speaks of a place in heaven called the 'Treasury of Merits', where people are being rewarded for their hardships by the treasures that are being placed into their crowns. Take note of the phase, 'crowns of life'.

> *"So, too, are there treasuries of comfort, where ministering angels sit and weave garments of salvation making crowns of life and fixing precious stones and pearls to them."*[96]

A heaven encounter reveals more,

> *"Crowns were hanging half-finished on hocks and along the shelves. Crates of precious gems and different metals waited for Him to turn them into something precious. 'Would you like to help me?' Jesus asked, 'Yes,' I said...He smiled, and before I could even pick up wire and get started, it appeared before me already bent into a circle, exactly what I had imagined, but without the stones. 'It isn't finished yet,' He said. It was then I realised we were working on my crown. 'With each new accomplishment, a new embellishment will be added to your crown, 'He said...All these crowns are for people still on earth. They are created over time as they experience different seasons and special moments in their lives. The crowns aren't completed*

---

[96] Howard Schwartz, Tree of Souls, Mythology of Judaism, Oxford University Press, 2004, p. 189

until their time on earth has passed... Each time I visit His worship, the crown has been added to, It is so beautiful, a moving living crown."[97]

The Crown of Life is not just a sign of a righteous life; it is your life manifesting above your head with the authority and experiences and glory you have become in Him. Your life story is the glory you will bring Him. Our living crown will be an eternal sign of our journey of life on earth and how we laid our lives down for our God. The children's visions through this book reveal the beauty of God's love towards us, that He is always walking with us, comforting us, even when most of us don't see Him face to face. The children's visions and encounters call us to walk lives worthy of our King Jesus. It matters how we live, as we are called to reflect Him and His likeness on earth. Our love and sacrifices will never be unnoticed, but greatly rewarded. Let us set our minds on things above, and rise to the high calling of God.

---

[97] Curtis, book 1, p. 87

The Apostles Foundation Stones

The New Jerusalem, is a 1500-mile cube of pure gold, like transparent glass. Its brilliance is like a very costly jasper stone. It has a high wall composed of jasper with twelve costly gates, three on each side of the city. An angel is stationed at each gate which is a single pearl engraved with one of the names of the tribes of Israel. The twelve foundation stones are engraved with the names of the apostles of the Lamb and adorned with every precious stone. The New Jerusalem, the City of God, is a spiritual manifestation of the bride of Christ built upon the apostles and Christ. Jewels are scattered on the foundation stones which have been engraved with the names of the twelve apostles of the Lamb. Each pearl gate is engraved with the names of the twelve tribes of Israel. This intentional interweaving of the apostles of Christ with the tribes of Israel shows the interdependence of all members of Christ upon another.[98]

Saints that overcome will also be engraved into the Temple/City,

> *"The one who is victorious I will make a pillar in the temple of my God. Never again will they leave it. I will write on them the name of my God and the name of the city of my God, the new Jerusalem, which is coming down out of heaven from my God; and I will also write on them my new name." (Revelation 3:12)*

---

[98] Linda Cruz, p. 201

City of God Revealed

*"And the foundations of the wall of the city were garnished with all manner of **precious stones**. The first foundation was jasper; the second, sapphire; the third, a chalcedony; the fourth, an emerald; The fifth, sardonyx; the sixth, sardius; the seventh, chrysolite; the eighth, beryl; the ninth, a topaz; the tenth, a chrysoprasus; the eleventh, a jacinth; the twelfth, an amethyst." (Rev 19:20-21)*
*"O afflicted one, storm-tossed, and not comforted, Behold, I will set your stones in antimony, And your foundations I will lay in **sapphires**. "Moreover, I will make your battlements of **rubies**, And your gates of **crystal**, And your entire wall of **precious stones**.*
"All your sons will be taught of the Lord; And the well-being of your sons will be great.
"In righteousness you will be established; You will be far from oppression, for you will not fear; And from terror, for it will not come near you."
(Isaiah 54:11-14)

The entire context of Isaiah 54 is a description of the New Jerusalem.

The book of Tobit/Tobias (that was included in the Greek Septuagint) says,

> ***"For Jerusalem shall be built up with sapphires and emeralds, and precious stone:*** *thy walls and towers and battlements with pure gold. And the streets of Jerusalem shall be paved with beryl and carbuncle and stones of Ophir. And all her streets shall say, Alleluia; and they shall praise him, saying, Blessed be God, which hath extolled it for ever." (Tobit 13:16-18)*

Book of Enoch describes,

> *"I went from there to another place, and saw a mountain of fire flashing both day and night. I proceeded towards it; and perceived seven splendid mountains, which were all different from each other.* **Their stones were brilliant and beautiful; all were brilliant and splendid to behold; and beautiful was their surface…** *Three mountains were towards the east, and strengthened by being placed one upon another; and three were towards the south, strengthened in a similar manner There were likewise deep valleys, which did not approach each other And the* **seventh mountain was in the midst of them. In length they all resembled the seat of a throne, and odoriferous trees surrounded them…"** *(Enoch 24:1-2)*

The Seven Mountains

1 Enoch 17-19 describes Enoch's first journey through the heavens. In this first vision there are a number of scenes which depict an ancient world view which graphically imagines how the orderly universe is maintained. He sees the "high places" and storehouses of the earth where the rains and snows are kept. In Chapter 18 he sees the storehouse of the wind, the cornerstone of the earth, and the pillars of heaven. He also sees a "dark pit" with heavenly fire, described as a "desolate and terrible place."

> *"4. I saw the winds of heaven which turn and bring the circumference of the sun and all the stars to their setting. 5. I saw the winds on the earth carrying the clouds: I saw the paths of the angels. I saw at the end of the earth the firmament of the heaven above. And I proceeded and saw a place which burns day and night, where there are seven mountains of magnificent stones, three towards the east, and three towards the south. 7. And as for those towards the east, one was of coloured stone, and one of pearl, and one of **jacinth**, and those towards the south of red stone. 8. But the middle one reached to heaven like the throne of God, of alabaster, and the summit of the throne was of sapphire. 9. And I saw a flaming fire. And beyond these mountains 10, is a region the end of the great earth: there the heavens were completed. 11. And I saw a deep abyss, with columns of heavenly fire, and among them I saw columns of fire fall, which were beyond measure alike towards the height and towards the depth. 12. And beyond that abyss I saw a place which had no firmament of the heaven above, and no firmly founded earth beneath it: there was no water upon it, and no birds, but it was a waste and horrible place. 13. I saw there seven stars like great burning mountains, and to me, when I inquired regarding them, 14. The angel said: 'This place is the end of heaven and earth: this has become a prison for the stars and the host of heaven. 15.*

> *And the stars which roll over the fire are they which have transgressed the commandment of the Lord in the beginning of their rising, because they did not come forth at their appointed times. 16. And He was wroth with them, and bound them till the time when their guilt should be consummated (even) for ten thousand years."*

In 1 Enoch 24-25 Enoch is shown a huge mountain of fire. From there he could see seven other mountains made of precious stone and each more glorious than the next. The greatest of these summits is the throne on which God will sit "when he visits the earth with goodness" (25:3). On this mountain is a fragrant tree which no human has the authority to touch until the time of judgment. This is probably the Tree of Life from Paradise, similar to Revelation 22:2, 14 (*4 Ezra* 8:52). The fragrance of this tree will "penetrate their bones" and they will live a long life on the earth, "as you fathers lived in their days" (Some copies of 1 Enoch expand this to include "no sorrow, pain, torment, and plague shall not touch them", Isaac 26, note l). This is a significant passage in the first section of Enoch since it looks forward to a time when God will visit the earth and begin a period of peace.

Enoch is taken to the "centre of the earth" in Chapter 26, the city of Jerusalem (cf. Ezek. 5:5). A stream of water flows out of the holy mountain in several directions, similar to the description of the Temple in Ezekiel 47 and Revelation 22:1-5. From this vantage point he sees a desolate land with deep valleys and no trees growing in them. He asks the angel Uriel about this desolate land in Chapter 27. This is the place, the angel explains, where those who cursed the Lord and "utter hard words concerning the glory." A connection to the term is the use of the term *Gehenna* for hell.[99]

---

[99] https://readingacts.com/2016/06/06/enochs-heavenly-journey-1-enoch-17-36/

WHEELS OF BERYL

In Ezekiel 10;8-9 it speaks about a mystical angelic chariot that has wheels within the wheels that sparkle like beryl stones. These angelic beings that seem to have wheels created in them are encased with gemstones.

> *"The cherubim appeared to have the form of a man's hand under their wings. And I looked, and behold, there were four wheels beside the cherubim, one beside each cherub, and the appearance of the wheels was like sparkling beryl."* (Ezekiel 10;8-9)

From Wikipedia, the free encyclopaedia it says,

> *"The **ophanim** (Hebrew: אוֹפַנִּים 'ōp̄annīm, 'wheels'; singular: אוֹפָן 'ōp̄ān), alternatively spelled **auphanim** or **ofanim**, and also called **galgalim** (Hebrew: גַּלְגַּלִּים galgallīm, 'spheres, wheels, whirlwinds'; singular: גַּלְגַּל galgal), refer to the wheels seen in Ezekiel's vision of the chariot (Hebrew merkabah) in Ezekiel 1:15–21. One of the Dead Sea scrolls (4Q405) construes them as angels; late sections of the Book of Enoch (61:10, 71:7) portray them as a class of celestial beings who (along with the Cherubim and Seraphim) never sleep, but guard the throne of God. In Christian angelology, they are one of the choirs (classes) of angels, and are also called **Thrones**.*
> *These "wheels" have been associated with Daniel 7:9 (mentioned as galgal, traditionally "the wheels of galgallin," in "fiery flame" and "burning fire") of the four, eye-covered wheels (each composed of two nested wheels), that move next to the winged Cherubim, beneath the throne of God. The four wheels move with the Cherubim because the spirit of the Cherubim is in them. The late Second Book of Enoch (20:1, 21:1) also referred to them as the "**many-eyed ones**".*

The First Book of Enoch (71.7) seems to imply that the Ophanim are equated to the "Thrones" in Christianity when it lists them all together, in order: "...round about were Seraphim, Cherubim, and Ophanim."[100]

---

[100] https://en.wikipedia.org/wiki/Ophanim

Christianity and Gems

Around the middle of the 3rd century AD gems engraved with Christian inscriptions and imagery first appeared in the Christian communities of the eastern Mediterranean. Identical to pagan gems in shape, material (usually cornelian, agate, or jasper), and engraving style, and likely produced by pagan gem cutters for their Christian clients, these gems bear distinctively Christian inscriptions or symbols, most notably the fish and the Good Shepherd. Soon afterward, narrative images were introduced, usually scenes from the Old Testament, such as Jonah and Daniel, which were given Christian interpretations. By the time the first Christian seals were introduced, however, the fashion for using engraved gems was waning. Although there was a brief revival under the Constantinian emperors, only a few workshops appear to have manufactured gems after the fourth century. One workshop produced fine garnets and sapphires at the end of the 5th century, and several distinctive groups of gems with religious iconography were cut in Asia Minor and Syria in the 5th and 6th centuries. In the East, within the Sasanian Empire (3rd to 7th centuries AD), where engraved gems remained very popular, the small Christian and Jewish communities also engraved seals.

Among the earliest Christian gems, datable to the mid-3rd century AD, are a number of small cornelians and jaspers engraved only with inscriptions naming or referring to Jesus Christ. Some read IHCOY XPICTOY, "of Jesus Christ" (in the genitive case, presumably meaning that the wearer was a "servant of Jesus Christ"), others merely IHCOY ("of Jesus") or XPICTOY ("of Christ"). Also used were the *chi-rho* monogram signifying "Christ" and the word IXQYC, meaning "fish" in

Greek but also a frequently used acrostic composed of the first letters of "Jesus Christ, Son of God, Saviour."

Another popular motif found on Christian gems of the later 3rd century is a pair of fish flanking an anchor or a cross-like object. Although the symbol is of pagan origin, attested first in the late Hellenistic period, its sudden appearance on gems in the 3rd century, as well as its occurrence in the Roman catacombs, demonstrates that Christians adopted the image, reinterpreting it as an allusion to Jesus (IXQYC). Some examples are labelled with explicitly Christian phrases.

Also appearing on gems of the later 3rd and 4th centuries is the image of the Good Shepherd. The shepherd is always shown carrying a sheep on his shoulders (the pose being that of the classical Greek *kriophoros*, but also a literal rendering of *Luke* 15:5), sometimes in a bucolic setting before a tree and with other sheep at his feet. Many of these gems have additional, explicitly Christian references, either inscriptions ("Jesus Christ," the *chi-rho* monogram, IXQYC, or some variant) or symbols, such as fish or anchors.

Some Old Testament figures, notably Jonah and Daniel, enjoyed special popularity with Christians, who viewed them as symbols of salvation, prefiguring or alluding to Jesus. On a number of gems, the Good Shepherd is paired with Daniel, who typically is represented as standing in the pose of an *orant* (in prayer) between two lions. Other gems show the cycle of abbreviated images illustrating the story of Jonah: Jonah cast from the ship, swallowed by the great fish (always depicted as the classical *ketos*, or sea-monster), vomited out by the *ketos*, and lying asleep under the gourds. Less frequently represented on gems, and perhaps slightly later in date (4th century AD) are other Old Testament figures, including Adam and Eve, Noah, and Abraham's sacrifice of his son Isaac. A further group of gems combines various images, such as the Good Shepherd, Jonah, Daniel, and Noah.

Only very few gems from the early Christian period (3rd to 5th centuries) survive that depict episodes from the New Testament. Surviving examples include representations of the Baptism of Jesus, the Raising of Lazarus, Peter and Paul, and three remarkable portrayals of the Crucifixion. The appearance of the Crucifixion on gems, in an unconventional composition which includes the twelve apostles, is significant for its early date, still in the 4th century if not earlier, for no other depiction of the Crucifixion is known until the 5th century.

A highly distinctive group of garnets and sapphires, all of identical shape, probably derive from a single workshop, perhaps in Constantinople. A number of these gems mounted in fine gold rings have been discovered in hordes of jewellery and gold coins, which can be firmly dated to the end of the 5th century AD. The most popular images on the garnets are doves, although peacocks, eagles, and dolphins also appear. Other examples are engraved with a new variety of Christian symbols and images, including representations of Jesus and the Virgin (standing as *orant*). From the same workshop are garnets and sapphires of identical shape engraved with personal monograms (in Greek) of early Byzantine type, sometimes accompanied by a cross.

A small number of gems of exceptional size and quality, all made of banded agate, may be products of an imperial workshop in Constantinople of 6th century date. Two examples in Munich (60 and 70 mm in length respectively) may have once been set in large gold fibulae of imperial Byzantine manufacture, surviving examples of which are set with unengraved stones of similar size and material. One agate depicts Christ enthroned, surrounded by the apostles, while the other shows a crowded scene of the twelve apostles standing before a large cross. An even larger agate (nearly 100 mm in length) in Vienna portrays Peter and Paul standing before a large cross above which is a bust of Christ and the inscription "Emmanuel".

A distinctive workshop, probably located in Syria, specialized in rock crystal gems engraved with episodes from the pictorial cycles of the life and miracles of Jesus. The large, oval gems, although engraved in a summary, linear style, were inlaid with gold foil, covered with another crystal and mounted in gold frames to be worn as pendants. Episodes from the life of Christ found on surviving examples comprise the Annunciation, Adoration, Baptism, Entry into Jerusalem, Crucifixion, Women at the Tomb, and Ascension. Miracle scenes include Changing the Water to Wine at Cana, the Healing of the Leper, the Healing of the Woman with the Issue of Blood, the Healing of the Blind Man, and the Raising of Lazarus. In addition, other rock crystals are engraved with images of Christ enthroned, angels, crosses, and saints. Several examples have been found in hoards which included Byzantine gold jewellery of late 6th or 7th century date. This short-lived workshop was among the last to produce gems before the iconoclastic movement of the 8th century finally put an end to the Graeco-Roman tradition of gem engraving.[101]

---

[101] Complete article – (accessed April 2024)
  https://www.carc.ox.ac.uk/carc/gems/Styles-and-Periods/Late-Antique-Early-Christian-and-Jewish

Birth Stones and the Bible

Birthstones, also known as "birthday stones, while the Bible does not mention birthstones, their widely accepted origin story has roots in biblical history. Exodus 28 contains instructions for making the sacred, priestly garments. Exodus 28:15–30 describes Aaron's high priestly breastplate, upon which 12 stones were used to represent the 12 tribes of Israel.

It describes the breastplate worn by Aaron, the first high priest of the Israelites, which was to be worn by all future high priests.

It wasn't until the first century, around 1500 years after Aaron's breastplate was described in the Book of Exodus, where the Jewish historian Josephus believed there to be a connection between the 12 stones in Aaron's breastplate, the 12 months of the year, and the 12 zodiac signs.

We see that the Bible does link humans to stars of which God names them all. We are also told Abraham's descendants were to be as the multitude of the stars.

> *"Therefore, from one man, and him as good as dead, were born as many as the stars of the sky in multitude - innumerable as the sand which is by the seashore." (Hebrews 11:12)*

God set the stars in the expanse of the sky to serve as signs, to mark seasons, days and years.

> *"Then God said, Let there be lights in the firmament of the heavens to divide the day from the night, and let them be for signs and seasons, and for days and years." (Genesis 1:14)*

The great Jewish historian Flavius Josephus (37-100 AD) in his book *Antiquities 5.2.5.7.* recounts the description of Aaron's breast piece:

> "Besides these, the High Priest put on a third garment, which was called the Ephod: which resembles the Epomis of the Greeks. Its make was after this manner. It was woven to the depth of a cubit, of several colours, with gold intermixed, and embroidered; but it left the middle of the breast uncovered. It was made with sleeves also. Nor did it appear to be at all differently made from a short coat. But in the void place of this garment there was inserted a piece of the bigness of a span, embroidered with gold, and the other colours of the Ephod. It is called Essen [the Breast-plate] which in the Greek language signifies the Oracle. This piece exactly filled up the void space in the Ephod.
>
> It is united to it by golden rings at every corner, the like rings being connected to the Ephod; and a blue ribband was made use of to tie them together by those rings; and that the space between the rings might not appear empty, they contrived to fill it up with stitches of blue ribbands. There were also two Sardonyxes upon the Ephod; at the shoulders, to fasten it, in the nature of buttons, having each end running to the Sardonyxes of gold, that they might be buttoned by them. On these were engraved the names of the sons of Jacob, in our own country letters, and our own tongue: six on each of the stones, on either side: and the elder sons names were on the right.
>
> Twelve stones also there were upon the breast-plate, extraordinary in largeness and beauty: and they were an ornament not to be purchased by men, because of their immense value. These stones however stood in three rows, by four in a row, and were inserted into the breast-plate itself, and they were set in ouches of gold, that were themselves inserted in the breast-plate: and were so made, that they might not fall out. Now the first three stones were, a sardonyx, a topaz, and an emerald. The second row contained a carbuncle, a jasper, and a sapphire. The first of the third row was a ligure, then an amethyst, and the third an agate; being the ninth of the whole number. The first of the fourth row was a chrysolite, the next was an onyx, and then a

beryl, which was the last of all. Now the names of all those sons of Jacob were engraven in these stones, whom we esteem the heads of our tribes; each stone having the honour of a name, in the order according to which they were born."

Josephus says, take note, *"...each stone having the honour of a name in the order according to which they were born."*

Here in Josephus' *Antiquities*, 1,500 years after the Book of Exodus in the Bible, we seem to have the first hint that perhaps each of the 12 stones on Aaron's Breast Plate gradually became the unique birth stone of people born in certain months. Can we take this concept further back in time?

If we start at the beginning of time, we see that we were chosen in the heavens, like a multitude of stars[102]. The 12 stars of the Zodiac came down as human precious stones being the leaders of the 12 tribes. The 12 tribes were grouped into four camps where all the early Israelites would be a part of one of them. Their births were recorded and placed on the Priests breastplate with physical precious stones. Their names were engraved on them as sons born in different months, and if applied to Genesis 1:14 in a spiritual sense, "all"[103] of us come down as a stone according to individual (seasons), days and years.[104]

---

[102] We came out of the womb of the dawn as morning stars. Yes, Scripture calls many "morning stars", Jesus the Great Morning star, angels and saints. A morning star is one who has shined in the light of creation as it was unfolding, while watching in eternity. Due to pre-existence we were there.

[103] Adam and Eve came down to earth first as a star and precious stone, then the rest of humanity came down in their due times, being born, their spirit being sent into their bodies at conception from God.

[104] We also see this in Ephesian 1:4, "He chose us in Him before the foundation of the world and predestined us into the earth to become sons."

The symbolism of the stars hints of where we came from and that is from above, and also when we were sent to earth to reflect on our month of birth, days and years. Did God not say, He had written our days in a book, the days fashioned for me, when as yet there were none of them? (Psalm 139:16), and that "He has determined our appointed times and the boundaries of our dwellings." (Acts 17:26)[105]

The Historian and Church Father Jerome, also referenced Josephus, and began to encourage the use of these stones by Christians in the 5th century. He even went on describing their therapeutic benefits when worn at specific times. Jerome's understanding of gemstones having therapeutic benefits in a way ties into the heaven stones being "living stones" with a frequency and emotion to heal creation.

According to the American Gem Society, these are the gems associated with each month.

January	-	Garnet
February	-	Amethyst
March	-	Aquamarine
April	-	Diamond
May	-	Emerald
June	-	Pearl (purity),
July	-	Ruby
August	-	Peridot, Sardonyx

---

[105] Ian Clayton says, "The veils objective is to give you the opportunity to understand the expanse of where you came from and where you came through to be here. According to Genesis One, You were positioned in the heavens as illuminations to give your light to the earth to rule over the day and night, to govern times and seasons, days and years prior to the sun and the moon and stars being put in their place. Your objective was to give light to the earth." The light (us) stores our record to produce matter, substance on the earth, so let your light shine.

September	-	Sapphire
October	-	Tourmaline, Opal
November	-	Topaz, Citrine
December	-	Tanzanite, Zircon, Turquoise

Another reason of evidence to believe in birth stones is that one of the children in the Orphanage in India in one of their daily heaven encounters was given ten stones by Jesus for her tenth birthday as a gift. As she came out of her heaven encounter, she opened her eyes, laying on the floor and in her hand, she saw that the stones had materialised on earth. They had come down through the veil as her spirit body fully returned to her physical body.

We read,

"On Chris's 10th birthday, she brought back from heaven 10 lightly coloured peridot stones, her birthstone. Jesus knows everything!"

If Jesus can make the link that others have grasped about birth stones, and can give the traditional chosen stone for her month then that is enough evidence for me.

Church Fathers and the Healing Benefits of Gemstones

Crystals have been used for centuries for their healing properties. In fact, many of the early church fathers wrote about the healing power of crystals. For example, Saint Basil the Great (4th century AD) wrote about how quartz crystals could be used to heal eye diseases. Saint Isidore of Seville (7th century AD) wrote about how amethyst could be used to prevent drunkenness.

> During the 12th to 14th centuries, members of the Christian clergy became interested in "lithotherapy" – the practice of using gemstones to heal the sick. The father of modern botany and zoology, Dominican monk Albertus Magnus (c. 1193-1280), was one of many serious scholars who dabbled in the study of lithotherapy. Sceptics were dismissed as heretics, and scholars who did not enthusiastically support tenets of lithotherapy were threatened with excommunication.[106]
>
> The idea that sapphires were beneficial for the eyes persisted through the Middle Ages. The Dominican monk, Albertus Magnus (1327-1377) recorded that he saw a sapphire remove a foreign body from the eye. In 1391, a sapphire was donated to St. Paul's Church in London by Richard-de-Preston, a grocer, so that it might cure the eye ailments of pious parishioners.[107]
>
> Early medieval writers believed that sapphires could reduce outbreaks of rage, dispel malicious behaviour, and repel envy. They were considered helpful for treating colic, mental illness,

---

[106] https://www.thenaturalsapphirecompany.com/education/sapphires-101/medicinal-properties-sapphires/

[107] https://www.thenaturalsapphirecompany.com/education/sapphires-101/medicinal-properties-sapphires/

and hysteria, and they were considered a good antidepressant.[108]

Thomas Aquinas's very comprehensive *Summa Theologica* did include a discussion of the wearing of substances in order to affect the body. Although Aquinas condemned the wearing of written characters and astrological images, he did admit that certain substances might have natural properties conferred on them by the stars which could affect the body.[109]

The healing capabilities of stones are referred to in both the *Talmud* and *Zohar*, indicating that the Patriarch Avraham (Abraham) had a healing stone which hung around his neck with which he was able to heal people **(Talmud Baba Basra16b).**

---

[108] https://www.thenaturalsapphirecompany.com/education/sapphires-101/medicinal-properties-sapphires/
[109] https://www.ncbi.nlm.nih.gov/pmc/articles/PMC4326677/#FN40

The Kingdom is the Present Future

The Kingdom is in the "Present Future." What do I mean by this statement. The Kingdom has arrived and is unfolding throughout creation until it has been renewed. The Scriptures tell us that the Kingdom realm has come to earth, is open and is joining with the earth in dimensions of reality, but also the Kingdom is still in heaven too. There is this tension of the "Present Future." Scripture also says, 'we have been saved, and are being saved, and will be saved.' The finished work is unfolding in the present as we walk out our destinies.

God being out-side time and heaven being in a different time realm to earth means that He can act out, fulfil "foretastes" of things to come in the earth now, which can also be described as future.

> *"And have tasted the good Word of God and the powers of the age to come." (Hebrews 6:5)*

Some may say that some Scriptures I use are future and I am stretching their meanings. For example, our works being judged as of precious stones, which is describing as a future event. But it is also true that it is also being "out worked" in the earth now and stones are being "formed" as a record and token. And yes, as a "foretaste" some are manifesting for people to behold.

I have learned from heaven revelation that this is the same with judgement day. We are told that all will be judged at the end of time, but God being outside the earths system of time (yes, He interacts continuously in it) that when a person dies, they are judged straight away in heaven. People are not all waiting for different periods of time in a holding place, some longer than others to be judged or rewarded. Here again we see this tension of the "Present Future."

Precious Stones in Blood

The Saint Philomena's remains were found in 1802 when workers stumbled over her grave. She was known to have died a martyr, and as the tradition was, a vial of her blood was buried beside her. As this vial of blood was looked at by many Church leaders, a visible chemical reaction happened in the blood, and gems, and flakes of gold and silver appeared in the vial. This substance was chemically tested over forty times and was confirmed to be human blood. Precious stones, rubies and emeralds, pieces of gold and flakes of silver have since appeared mingled with this blood in the vial. This chemical reaction, miracle has been seen many times, and this vial now lives in the Sanctuary of St. Philomena located in Mugnano, Italy.[110]

---

[110] Fr. Paul O Sullivan, Saint Philomena; The Wonder Worker, Lisbon; Catholic Printing Press, Rockford, Illinois; Tan, 1993, p.42

Stones as Beacons of Frequency!

From God's throne on the Mountain flows living water a fountain (Jeremiah 17:12-14). The fountain flows into a river in to a crystal sea. Flowing out of God are precious stones like tokens of His creative works. The stones build up and turn the sea crystal shining with many colours. From the sea the stones flow down under the throne, under the heavenly temple and down in the spirit of the four rivers. The river of God is the spirit of God and this river can flow anywhere behind the veil (in the spiritual world resting behind the physical world- bringing life). This river is the "river of life" and where ever it flows it brings life.

We are told of God's River/Spirit that it will bring comfort, healing and transformation to the earth as heaven joins the earth.

> *"For the Lord will comfort Zion, He will comfort all her waste places. He will make her wilderness like Eden, And her desert like the garden of the Lord." (Isaiah 51:3)*

As God's creative works are recorded in precious stones pouring out of the throne into the river they hold a frequency of creative glory. As God acts in the earth these living stones flow down from the heavenly river all through creation where He is praised and worshipped. These living stones are like "beacons" in the earth that live behind the veil giving of frequencies of different aspects of God's redeeming powers. Some bring healing to creation; they heal because they are living stones formed in the river of life out of the God of Life. Others bring angels to position their guard, others are churches treasures, gifts, authorities, mantles, ownership of territories. As I have mentioned some of these stones will manifest as a foretaste.

Heaven is full of gemstones everything is encrusted with stones. In the walls, in the trees[111], in petals of flowers, on pathways, in streams, houses, in crowns, you name it, its pulsating in heaven. The living stones as they fall to earth behind the veil are influencing change, but they also will one day "all" come through making earth look like heaven with the frequency of heaven in a record of God's creative work. The stones are a part of 'creative things' their DNA of which God weaves into the things He makes. Every creative thing/object has its testimony and record of life.

> *"As the new heavens and the new earth that I make will endure before me." (Isaiah 66:22)*

The idea of gemstones giving off frequencies is not strange or New Age (although they do use them). Crystals are known to give off a very high frequency. Crystals have a super stable energy frequency that doesn't change.

---

[111] Interesting to note in, The Epic of Gilgamesh, it speaks of a tree in Paradise that bears precious gems (tablet 9).

Jesus Was Well Aware of Heaven Stones

Having read this book this far I think one will agree that heaven stones are a reality and the Bible does talk about them. One question someone may ask is did Jesus talk about them and did he have an awareness of them coming down from heaven. Also, can this be grounded by tradition and the Bible. I believe that it can and Jesus was well aware of heaven stones in his own words.

Jesus was well grounded in the Old Testament (it is written he said often) and he knew that precious stones came down from heaven in the spirit/river into the garden of Eden (Gen 2:10-11). The stones came down to the garden from the crystal sea around the throne.

> "A river flowed out of Eden to water the garden, and from there it separated and became four heads. The name of one is Pishon; that is the one that encompasses all the land of Havilah, where there is gold. The gold of that land is good; there is the crystal and the onyx stone."

The bdellium is a precious stone, which the Jewish writers (a) commonly take to be crystal; and, according to Solinus (b), the best crystal is in Scythia. Bochart (c) would have it that the pearl is meant, because of its whiteness and roundness.

Jesus knew of the Ocean of Tears on God's Mountain-

> "Your love, Oh Lord, reaches to the heavens, your faithfulness to the skies. Your righteousness is like the mighty mountain, your justice like the great ocean. Oh Lord, you preserve man and beast... Therefore, the children of men

put their trust under the shadow of your wings."
(Psalms 36:5-7)

Jesus knew what the priests breast plate meant and what the stones functions represented. Jesus knew Father God and that the priest's breastplate was a symbolic copy of the skin of the Father's body inlaid with sapphire stones. He knew of the tablets of stone that came down and of the Urim & Thummim that were not of this world.

Jesus knew Isaiah 45:3, "I will give you hidden treasure, riches stored in secret places, so that you may know that I AM the Lord, the God of Israel, who summons you by name."

Jesus used "stone" terminology to describe anyone who put their faith in him as being a little stone (Peter), and then we see this explained more in calling us living stones a spiritual temple being built up. One must ask why did Jesus use stone theology? It is because he knew we were treasure hidden in him from the foundation of the world. In calling us living stones of a spiritual temple he places us above and gives significance behind the veil and in the spiritual Kingdom. He makes a comparison between us and precious stones.

Jesus in heaven showed Paul in a vision (in the book of Revelation) all around heaven, seeing precious stones in heaven, the New Jerusalem and also Jesus gave the warnings to the seven churches, one being that 'to him who overcomes he would give hidden manna and a precious stone with a new name.' Jesus knew about the crystal sea and stones forming in the river from the throne.

Jesus gives a Parable about hidden treasure in a field and of a great pearl (Matthew 13:44-46). Why did Jesus use this "terminology" of hidden treasure and pearls? Most likely because he was drawing on Jewish tradition and realities of precious stones, manna and pearls coming (raining) down in the wilderness for the tabernacle (heaven stones).

> "Again the Kingdom of heaven is like treasure hidden in a field, which a man found and hid, and for joy over it he goes and sells all that he has and buys that field." (Matthew 13:44)

The Catholic Scholar Stephen Beale says, "Moreover, according to ancient Jewish tradition, precious stones and pearls rained down from heaven along with the manna."

The Targum Yonason says, "that heavenly clouds brought the stones from the Pishon River to the wilderness."

The Midrash Exodus Rabb, chapter 33 says, - "Along with the manna which fell for Israel in the desert and provided them sustenance, precious stones and Jewels fell. The leaders of Israel came and gathered them and stored them for the tabernacle."

Even if these accounts were written down later, they were known from the time period and passed on as oral tradition.

Did Jesus use the terms by chance or because he was now the true temple/tabernacle. If God rained down heavenly stones in the wilderness, would He not do it again in His Kingdom over His Church. The Parable does not say he dug for treasure; it says he found hidden treasure. Could this treasure be precious stones that had come down hidden behind the veil that had now come through to be found in the field - the unseen had become substance (Hebrews 11:1). These stones, treasures brought much joy at the reality of the Kingdom so the man in the Parable hid them in a safe place and went and sold all he had because he had found that they revealed the true and greatest pearl - God. The man surrendered his whole life to the Kingdom and God.

In the other parables, the feast is real, the wedding is real, why not the hidden treasure?

David Wenham in his book, The Parables of Jesus, says, "In the parable of Jesus a man, perhaps a hired labour, found such a cache, maybe a jar containing silver coins or jewels."

Why would Jesus use these terms if they had no connection to stones of the spiritual Kingdom – crystal sea, river into Eden, tablets of stone, Urim and Thummim, heaven stones, precious stones, manna, pearls.

Even Jesus had the connection, the link that he would give overcomer's hidden manna and a white stone (Rev 2:17) in good awareness that manna and stones came down from heaven. Some may try and say, but it just says one stone, but Scripture also says, our works will be as precious stones (1 Corinthian 3:12).

Attitudes of the Heart

> *"Again, the Kingdom of heaven is like treasure hidden in a field, which a man found and hid, and for joy over it he goes and sells all that he has and buys that field." (Matthew 13:44)*

There is always a cost and a reward to those who keep seeking and stay open minded and grateful to God's signs and wonders and treasures.

A Jewish Folklore says,

> *"A bumpkin who prays to God to send him treasure from heaven finds a jar in the field. Inside are precious stones, but he covers it up, annoyed that the gift is from the earth and not from heaven. The man whom he alerts to the jar of precious stones finds only a snake inside, Angry, sure that the bumpkin was trying to kill him, the man climbs on the roof of the bumpkin's house. He shakes out the snake, but gold and diamonds fall."*[112]

This Jewish folklore speaks to the attitudes of one's heart. The bumpkin man prays for heavenly treasure, then finds treasure in the field, but disregards God's gift from heaven as being just earthly looking. Another man who was alerted about the jar goes to check out the jar, but only finds a snake in it.

Both were angry, but had different heart attitudes. When the man who only found a snake in the jar climbs on the roof to shake the snake out - to his amazement he finds only gold and diamonds fall out. God had answered the bumpkins request, but his disregard of the stones made him miss out. God changed the stones into a snake. Then when the other man went to check on

---

[112] Pinhus Sadeh

the jar, he only found a snake, but kept seeking. For when he went to shake the snake out once he had climbed on the roof and taken the lid off, God had replaced the stones in the jar and removed the snake.

We must be careful how we judge God's gifts and how we assume He must answer.

Jason Cobb reveals that he has received many different types of stones with different grades and qualities and values all from God.

> *"Over the years we have seen different quality stones come through: -*
> *1. Precious i.e. diamonds (valuable according to earth standards)*
> *2. Glass / crystal / common (no real earth value)*
> *3. Plastic / nylon (these cause the most offence as people can't relate these to God & Heaven)*
> *These also have different weight levels, heavy to light.*
> *Rejection or acceptance of heaven stones often comes when people see a lesser substance/ value/ weight/ grade (according to earth standards). I've often thought that these levels are also part of a heart test.[113]"*

God watches the human heart and its motives and looks for gratefulness. A gift is a gift and must be accepted as a gift with no earthly self-promotion goals or requirements.

Jesus did say, "Do not lay up for yourselves treasure on earth, where moth and rust destroy and where thieves break in and steal. But lay up for yourselves treasure in heaven, where neither moth nor rust destroys and where thieves do not break in and steal. For

---

[113] In a private conversation.

where your treasure is, there your heart will be also." (Matthew 6:19-21)

* That is do not run after earthly treasure and material wealth that can be an idol or stolen or left to rust.

* But lay up for yourselves heavenly treasure (of which stones are a token of heavenly rewards, gifts and greater glory dimensions) that will be seen above.

* For where your treasure is there your heart will be. If your treasure is out of heaven, stored in heaven it will reveal that your focus and heart is in God's heart-beat.

A seer friend recalls seeing angels bring stones on plates and position them behind the veil for people to find. They saw them shake their wings and precious stones fell out for people to gather as they slowly appeared. They watched the angels tap people's hands and knock the stones out if they didn't belong to that person who picked it up. They even saw stones disappear when the heart of the person wasn't in the right place to accept that wonderful treasure. Some looked for the earthly value of heaven stones and what it could bring them, maybe wealth, fame, promotion, and a heart of pride...[114]

From the very first page of this book, I have showed that "we" came out of God as sapphire stones. I now end this part of the book showing that "we" will be God's polished and devoted sapphire stones serving in His eternal Kingdom. The Key definition for Sapphire is, "polishing" to be polished, and the Key definition for the name Nazarite is, "A consecrated one who is devoted."

---

[114] Reworded - Angela Curtis, p.100

"Her Nazarites were purer than snow, they were whiter than milk, they were ruddier in body than rubies, and their polishing was of sapphire." (Lamentations 4:7)

Objections From Critics

Below are objections that people give to the manifestation of heaven stones.

* The stones have no reference to Biblical truth? This is not true as my book has shown.
* Jesus never knew of gemstones? This is also false and I have shown otherwise.
* Does the Bible talk of unusual miracles? "The LORD does whatever pleases him, in the heavens and on the earth, in the seas and all their depths." (Psalm 135:6)
* The stones drive people away from God? The evidence has been from many the complete opposite, they are drawn deeper in intimacy with God due to an explosion of faith of the realness of God and His love. Yes, some people do have wrong motives and the Bible warns about heart issues. We could also say that those who raise the issue are jealous they haven't received a stone.
* Half these stones are not valuable so they are not from God? A gift is a gift and given to the spiritual age one deserves often. The value of the stone or its material does not discredit the giver (God).
* Why don't people get very valuable stones? Some people do, but the stones go from glory to glory, from light to heavy, depending on one's spiritual character, heart and mantle/gifting. Authority and power is not given to all or to unstable people or people who would stumble often. A simple stone for many is enough to open the door to greater faith.
* If gold and precious stones can appear from God, why does He not give them to the starving in Africa? God does give through many avenues, through people, through

donations, through missionaries, food multiplications, and just maybe if someone was to pray for one God could/would give them one. But the stones are part of a spiritual Kingdom, not a wealth system that people's hearts could most likely use in a wrong motive. They are not an earthy monetary system; they are part of a spiritual inheritance and some are gifts.
* What do gemologists or geologists find when they test these stones? Again, some are precious stones, diamonds, emeralds, others are semi-precious, some are just gemstones, others cubic zirconia (man-made looking diamonds), some glass transparent looking, and some even plastic looking. Some stones come with writing inside them too. Trying to judge from what type of stone it is – if it is God will not work. God is always using mystery. Take a Cubic Zirconia diamond, which humans can make. But didn't God create every substance on earth? and put every invention in the minds of humans to make all things. Can He not use the same process and drop them from the air? with also adding writing inside them?
* God doesn't need to give every one precious stones, and He checks the heart for offences. People are too quick to judge if a stone is real or not depending on its makeup. This is not the best way to determine their realness, yes it would be an easy way, but it is not conclusive.

Ed Rocha in his book, *Angels – God's Supernatural Agents*, endorsed by Bill Johnson, recalls gems appearing and being tested by a geologist,

> *"It is common for gems to appear around people when I am leading worship or praying for healing. Not long ago I was ministering at a church in Sao Paulo, Brazil, and precious stones started to manifest around me and around the people I was praying for. Many people were healed that night. A couple*

of weeks ago I was preaching in our church, Pier49, in Rio, Brazil. His thick presence (God's) filled the air, it was so precious and tangible. It did not take long for precious stones and gold specks to start manifesting all around us. Diamonds, emeralds, amethysts and gold specks started to fall from heaven on us as we stood there in worship.

"Stones were taken to a geologist and they were amazed at the quality of the real stones. This geologist said that although the specific gravity of the stones he was testing did not match any stones he had ever seen in nature, they were real gemstones - not synthetic ones like cubic zirconia.

The geologist also said that the clarity of the stones was unique. All the real gems he tested were translucent, with fine colour, except for the colourless diamonds. There hardness did not match any stones he had ever seen or studied. In the natural, the hardness (scratch resistance) of precious gems ranges from 1-10. The opal family, for example, ranges around 5-6, while the emeralds family ranges around 7-8. Diamonds measure 10 on the hardness scale, which is why tiny diamonds are used in glass cutting tools.

According to the geologist, however, all the real gems that were tested measured above 11 in their hardness, which makes no sense to him. Other technical and geological specifications in the heaven-sent gems did not match that of regular precious stones on the market, either."[115]

* I have seen documentation from a guy called Jason Cuellar, who took his gemstones to a gemmologist to silence critics, who confirmed all were real stones and had a price value of $3500.
* Jeff Jansen had (since died) stones appear in his meetings, that have been tested and are cut so perfect they are believed to be not of this world, meaning not seen before like this (50 Carat Rubies).

---

[115] Ed Rocha, "Angels–God's Supernatural Agents" Chosen Books (April 4, 2017)

* The Gateway Fellowship Church (documented in this book); Rick Hurt has had a few professional gem buyers and sellers have a look at their stones but the findings are inconclusive. "The specific gravity of these stones does not match anything in nature. The specific gravity ranged from 5.9 sg to 6.4 sg. The sizes of the stones were perplexing at 45 to 55 carets. He had looked into artificial stones but found that they were large even for man-made stones and that manufactured stones of that size are typically foggy.

    He finally concluded that he was going to continue to try to identify the stones and maybe send them to a government lab but concluded "I don't know if we ever will know for sure. It may be that we don't need to know anything more than where they came from."

* What do Jewellers say? I know of one interesting account where a family I know personally prayed for a heaven stone at home for a future wedding ring. A stone manifested and it was taken to a jeweller to put in a ring. The stone was a Cubic Zirconia Diamond ...The jeweller asked, "Where did you get this stone from? This is very old. Its cut is intricate and very unique. This stone is not from our generation, but from the past. It has a royal cut from the early 1900s. Plus it looks like something is written in a different language right inside the stone." The jeweller was baffled and couldn't understand - 1. Where they got the stone from, and 2. How it had writing in it. For some because it was seen as a Cubic Zirconia Diamond, they might already be judging a conclusion in their mind, but this stone appeared from prayer out of a person's hand from a heaven encounter. The stone also has the nick name of the other spouse written in the stone of which they couldn't do. Again, we see mystery in the ways God does things, this stone is a very precious stone.

The Jeweller analysed that the stone was a cubic zirconia because under his microscope testing equipment it revealed no blemishes (which earth diamonds always reveal) so it must have been made in a controlled lab environment.[116]

* The stones baffle and mystify! Michael King shares an experience of a friend,
  "We have had gems tested, and when different people brought the same gem into the jeweller, he got different results based on what the person who brought the stone believed about the stone."

It also is not all about the quality, or I should say the substance of the stones. What makes many of these stones very different to earthly stones is they appear falling out the sky often or in hands in heaven trances, or just out of thin air, and also is the fact that these stones are alive! They are living stones. These stones often when they appear glow, pulsate with presence, even grow before people eyes. Some even disappear before your eyes; I have never seen natural stones do this!

I can remember going to Germany with a few of my stones on me. These were glassy ones, and at this large conference, I pulled them out to show two Pastors. The stones in my hand came alive, pulsating with presence. As one of the Pastors put his hand over my hand, he was slain on the floor by the presence of God on the stones.

---

[116] From the jewellers perspective and beliefs the stone because it had no blemishes had to fit into his box of thinking that it was man made looking, but God can make a stone that has no blemishes in it.

* Some stones have been shown to gemologists and they have said straight up these are glass jewels, and these are stones that appeared out of thin air in heavy presence.

Len Lacroix in Hungary documented in this book,

"I spoke by phone with my Christian cousin, back in the States, who is a certified gemologist. I told him about these and he said that if I place the stones face down on a printed page, such as a magazine, and can read the text, then they are not diamonds. He said that when it is a diamond, you couldn't read the text through the stone. He asked me to take a photo and send it to him. I took the photos and some video footage of it to send to my cousin. He wrote back saying his first impression is that these are glass jewels."

* David from California, took a perfectly cut diamond that appeared during prayer to a gemologist. After studying the flawless stone, he offered them $10,000 for it.
* I have also seen another gemologists appraisal report from a man called Carl Meyerdirk, who posted it online. He took it to 'Sissy's Log Cabin' - 1825 North Grant Street, Little Rock, AR 72207. Their showroom includes an extraordinary selection of designer jewellery, engagement rings, watches and more.
The appraisal reads, - "Amethyst - This 270.0 carat, round mixed cut purple amethyst with medium dark tone and strong saturation measures 46.37 x 21.10 mm. One side of the gem features checker-board faceting and the other side is brilliant cut. The gem has very good polish and very good symmetry. - Value $5400"
* Glenn Smith took a unique stone to a gemologist who said it was a geological impossibility. The heart-shaped stone features four completely different stones, amethyst, heliodor, pink sapphire, and emerald, with all four fused together as one.

The stones will always bring mystery, and baffle many and even offend, but for those who in His presence receive them with a humble heart they are a gift of awe that changes them.

Don't Cast Your Pearls

Like everything in life wisdom must be used in all conversations in sharing Kingdom truths. The stones from heaven are a powerful witness, but discernment must be used to whom you share the knowledge of the stones with. Discernment is also called for in who you show the stones too.

Jesus warned that not everyone would be as open or as excited as we are in the mystical teachings of the Kingdom. In their harsh judgements they defile truth. We are called not to stir trouble where trouble is not needed or let these beautiful gifts be robbed of their glory by their responses. I can understand why the Lord makes some stones in a crowd disappear before "some" people - so they can't pick them up.

> *"Do not give dogs what is sacred, do not throw your pearls to pigs. If you do, they may trample them under their feet, and turn and tear you to pieces."*
> *(Matthew 7:6)*

Jesus uses strong words, calling certain character traits (people) dogs or pigs. Untrained dogs tend to snap and pigs make a mess in the mud like defilement of clean robes.

The passage *"do not throw your pearls to pigs. If you do, they may trample them under their feet, and turn and tear you to pieces."* was explained by the church father Origen as signifying that "the pearls are the more mystical teachings of God, and the swine those who roll in impiety and in all kinds of pleasures, as swine do in mud. For he said that, by these words of Christ not to cast about divine teachings, in as much as they could not bear them who were held by impiety and brutal pleasures."

I like how Origen relates the word "pearls" to mystical teachings! - it fits perfect with heaven stones.

The church father Clement of Alexandria said, "Even now I fear 'to cast the pearls before swine…' For it is difficult to display the truly pure and transparent words about true light to swinish and untrained hearers. For, to the multitude, hardly anything that they hear could seem more ludicrous." (195 AD)

Church Fathers;
Rock of the Soul

Jesus is the eternal Rock that came down to earth, the chief corner stone of the spiritual temple. The temple has other members, his body, that must awake by faith to where they came from and join the foundation as precious rocks (stones).

> *"For no other foundation can anyone lay that that which is laid, which is Jesus Christ." (1 Corinthians 3:11)*
> *"For they drank of that spiritual Rock that followed them, and that Rock was Christ." (1 Corinthians 10:4)*
>
> *Jesus said to them, "But who do you say that I 'am? Peter answered and said, "The Christ of God." (Luke 9:20)*
>
> *"Jesus answered and said to him, 'Blessed are you, Simon Bar-Jonah, for flesh and blood has not revealed this to you, but My Father who is in heaven. And I also say to you that you are Peter, and on this rock, I will build My church, and the gates of hell shall not prevail against it." (Matthew 16:17- 18)*

Those that come to faith are said to be members, rocks (stones) of the spiritual temple. Not only Peter, but all who confess Jesus is the Christ are called rocks or precious stones (1 Peter 2:4-5). Jesus said to Simon- you are Petra, which means a little stone.

> *"Coming to Him as to a living stone, rejected by men, but chosen by God and precious, you also, as living stones, are being built up a spiritual house, a holy priesthood, to offer up spiritual sacrifices acceptable to God through Jesus Christ." (1 Peter 2:4-5)*

Jesus came to save us and raise us up to the Rock we came from, the Father through the Son. Our souls are rocks, precious stones being polished to shine God's light. Everything we do with a pure heart brings forth treasure in heaven and on earth manifesting gemstones (gems) into the atmosphere of the earth, behind the veil and through it to leave a token of glory.

Basil the Great (370 AD)

"The soul of the blessed Peter was called a lofty rock because he had a strong mooring in the faith."

Jerome (350 AD)

"The rock is Christ, Who gave to His apostles that they also should be called rocks, "Thou art Peter, and upon this rock I will build My Church."

Aphaates (280 AD)

"Thus also the true stone, our Lord Jesus Christ is the foundation of all faith. And on Him, on (this) stone faith is based. And resting on faith all structures rise until it is completed. For it is the foundation that is the beginning of all the building. For when anyone is brought nigh unto faith, it is laid for him upon the stone, that is Jesus Christ."

Augustine (350 AD)

"Thou art Peter, and upon this rock I will build my Church, that it be understood as built upon Him whom Peter confessed."

Origen (250 AD)

"And if we too have said like Peter, 'Thou art the Christ, the Son of the living God,' not as if flesh and blood had revealed it

unto us, but by light from the Father in heaven having shone in our hearts, we become a Peter, and to us there might be said by the Word, 'Thou art Peter', For a rock is every disciple of Christ of whom those drank, who drank of the spiritual rock which followed them, and upon every such rock is built every word of the church."

Ambrose (350 AD)

"Make an effort, therefore to be a rock! Do not seek the rock outside of yourself, but within yourself. Your rock is your deed, your rock is your mind. Upon this rock your house is built Your rock is your faith, and faith is the foundation of the Church. If you are a rock, you will be in the Church, because the Church is on a rock. If you are in the Church the gates of hell will not prevail against you."

Origen (250 AD)

"Now Paul says this also to me, in order that I not build in a careless way, since I know that on that day the fire will test what sort of work I build. I take care in building not to add on wood, hay, or straw. For if I carelessly add wicked souls to the church, I have attached to the good foundation, Christ Jesus, wood, and others who are hay, and others who are straw. On the other hand, it will be clear that I have built precious stones upon the foundation if some who belong to the building shine brilliantly— and so brilliantly that they are like those stones in the description of Jerusalem and the temple: chosen stones and stones of crystal and stones of sapphire and all the other stones named there (Isa 54:11–12; Rev 21:19–21). The temple of God (1 Cor 3:16) and the building of God (1 Cor 3:9) are to have gold like the temple that Solomon built as the archetype of a temple that has much gold and silver (1 Kings 6:20–22). Thus if someone else comes and builds, the gold he adds to the building will prove *to be more precious than the silver. I myself must take care: I do not wish that through me wood and hay and straw should be introduced. Even if I am considered worthy of salvation on other grounds (since Paul writes, he himself will be saved, but only as through fire), it is not my wish—wretched man that I am (Rom 7:24)—that I be saved in such a way as to fill the building with wood, hay, and straw, through not being receptive to grace and not building well. This is not what God's word intends. For the fire will test what sort of work each one has done...."*

> *"For no other foundation can anyone lay than that which is laid, which is Jesus Christ. Now if anyone builds on this foundation with gold, silver, precious stones, wood, hay, straw, each one's work will become clear; for the day will declare it, because it will be revealed by fire; and the fire will test each one's work, of what sort it is. if anyone's work which he has built on it endures, he will receive a reward. If anyone's work is burned, he will suffer loss, but himself will be saved, yet so as through fire. Do you not know that you are the temple of God and the spirit of God dwells in you?" (1 Corinthians 3:11-16)*

The Scriptures

God is the eternal stone: Jasper, Sardius, Cornerstone, Capstone.

> *"And He who sat there was like a Jasper and Sardius stone in appearance, and there was a rainbow around the throne, in appearance like an emerald." (Revelation 4:3)*

> *"Therefore, thus says the Lord God, Behold, I lay in Zion a stone for a foundation. A tried stone, a precious cornerstone, a sure foundation." (Isaiah 28:16)*

> *"And he shall bring forth the capstone with shouts of 'grace, grace' to it." (Zecheriah 4:7).*

> *"His hands are rods of gold, set with beryl. His body is carved ivory inlaid with sapphires. His legs are pillars of marble set on bases of fine gold." (Song of Songs 5:14)*

God, the eternal stone sits on a Sapphire Throne.

> *"And I looked. And there in the firmament that was above the head of the cherubim there appeared something like a sapphire stone, having the appearance of the likeness of a throne." (Ezekiel 10:1)*

> *"And He showed me a pure river of water of life, clear as crystal, proceeding from the throne of God and of the Lamb." (Revelation 22:1)*

A rainbow shines over the Throne reflecting seven stones:
> **Ruby – red;**
> **Jacinth – orange;**
> **Topaz – yellow;**
> **Emerald – green;**
> **Chalcedony – blue;**
> **Sapphire – indigo;**
> **Amethyst – violet.**

> *"Like the appearance of a rainbow in a cloud on a rainy day, so was the appearance of the brightness all around it. This was the appearance of the likeness of the Lord."*
> *(Ezekiel 1:28)*

In God, there is the breath of life, the spirit of wisdom, perfection, and knowledge; the eternal stone shines forth His Spirit.

> *"The Mighty One, God the Lord, has spoken and called the earth from the rising of the sun to its going down. Out of Zion, the perfection of beauty, God will shine forth, and shall not keep silent. A fire shall devour before Him, and it shall be very tempestuous all around Him."*
> *(Psalms 50:1-3)*

> *"For the Lord gives Wisdom, from His mouth come knowledge and understanding."* (Proverbs 2:6)

> *"But we speak the wisdom of God in a mystery, the hidden mystery which God ordained before the ages for our glory."*
> *(1 Corinthians 2:7)*

In the eternal stone, there was from the foundation of the world, treasure hidden and given into the Son's name and ownership.

> *"In Christ Jesus is hidden all the treasures of wisdom and knowledge" (Colossians 2:3)*
>
> *"Just as He chose us in Him before the foundation of the world, that we should be holy..." (Ephesians 1:4)*
>
> *"For every good gift and every perfect gift is from above and comes down from the Father of Lights with whom there is no variation or shadow of turning. Of His own will He brought us forth by the word of truth, that we might be a kind of first fruit of His creatures." (James 1:17-18)*
>
> *"Coming to Him as to a living stone rejected indeed by men, but chosen by God and precious, you also, as living stones, are being built up a spiritual house, a holy priesthood, to offer up spiritual sacrifices acceptable to God through Jesus Christ."*
> *(1 Peter 2:4-5)*

The eternal mystery of the ages was that in God, His living stones would be chosen and predestined from the foundation of the world to reflect the nature of God going from glory to glory. In God, His light, His presence shines the fullness of wisdom through His living stones, and as they reflect like precious stones, the fullness of wisdom, beauty, and knowledge is revealed to the universe. In fact, the mystery was to show forth this truth to the principalities and powers in the Heavenly places.

> *"And to make all see what is the fellowship of the mystery, which from the beginning of the ages has been hidden in God, who created all things through Jesus Christ, to the intent that now the manifold wisdom of God might be made known by the church to the principalities and powers in the Heavenly places according to the eternal purpose which he accomplished in Christ Jesus our Lord."*
> *(Ephesians 3:9-11)*

Before the Throne, are the seven spirits of God that manifest various facets of wisdom and revelation.

> *"The Spirit of the Lord will rest on him, the spirit of wisdom and understanding, the spirit of counsel and strength, the spirit of knowledge and the fear of the Lord." (Isaiah 11:2)*

> *"Grace to you and peace from Him who is and who was and who is to come, and from the seven spirits who are before His throne." (Revelation 1:4)*

There is also a correlation between the nine spiritual gifts and the seven spirits of God: Word of Wisdom, Word of Knowledge, Discerning of Spirits, Tongues, Interpretation of Tongues, Prophecy, Faith, Working of Miracles, and Gifts of Healing.

Over the Throne, there was the anointed cherub who covered God's presence. Lucifer was able to look into God and see the one "who is and who was and who is to come."

> *"You were the anointed cherub who covers, I established you. You were on the holy mountain of God, You walked back and forth in the midst of fiery stones." (Ezekiel 28:14)*

> *"Grace to you and peace from Him who is and who was and who is to come, and from the seven Spirits who are before His throne." (Revelation 1:4)*

Lucifer had the seal of perfection, beauty, and wisdom because he covered the full presence of God. As Lucifer walked amidst the stones of fire in the heart of God, the stones vibrated the secrets of God's nature, shining as living stones. As Lucifer yielded his heart into God's heart, physical precious stones were placed into Lucifer's breastplate as a seal of perfection.

> *"You were the seal of perfection, full of wisdom and perfect in beauty. You were in Eden, the garden of God. Every precious stone was your covering, the sardius, topaz, and diamond, beryl, onyx, and jasper, sapphire, turquoise, and emerald with gold." (Ezekiel 28:13)*

> *"Out of Zion, the perfection of beauty, God will shine forth, and shall not keep silent. A fire shall devour before Him, and it shall be very tempestuous all around Him." (Psalms 50:1-3)*

Lucifer covered the Throne of God and His presence, and I believe he also saw Believers in God's heartbeat. Lucifer got his perfection and beauty from reflecting God's presence, and was constructed inwardly so that his very breathing produced music (like pipes) (Ezekiel 28:13) as he yielded to the breath of God. He also covered in the sense of having nine precious stones on him, which filtered the revelation of God's glory throughout the heavens.

Lucifer had nine precious stones upon him, covering stones, these were to reflect the manifold wisdom of God and the nine gifts of the spirit.

> *"Every precious stone was your covering, the sardius, topaz, and diamond, beryl, onyx, and jasper, Sapphire, turquoise, and emerald with gold." (Ezekiel 28:13)*

Once Lucifer had seen the mystery of the ages in God, that it would be Believers who would shine forth the manifold fullness of God's image, he became corrupt, and jealousy rose in his heart that mankind would be greater than his image. So, he set out to set himself up as God and went out to trade us, living stones to be his.

In this battle, he rebelled in his heart and took a third of the angels with him, and God threw him out of Heaven. Lucifer could not stand the concept that a people would shine forth in the beauty of grace and perfection.

Because of Lucifer's heart and hatred, the Jewels (Believers) are at the centre of cosmic conflict. From the very beginning, Lucifer's heart has been to trade us, to own us, and use our gifts to be used for himself and our destruction.

> *"By the abundance of your trading, you became filled with violence within, and you sinned. Therefore, I cast you as a profane thing out of the mountain of God, and I destroyed you, O covering cherub, from the midst of the fiery stones. Your heart was lifted up because of your beauty, You corrupted your wisdom for the sake of your splendour." (Ezekiel 28:16-17)*

> *"You surely shall not die! For God knows that in the day you eat from it, your eyes will be opened, and you will be like God, knowing good and evil." (Genesis 3:4-5)*

> *"Then Jesus was led up by the Spirit into the wilderness to be tempted by the devil." (Matthew 4:1)*

> *"Be sober, be vigilant, because your adversary, the devil, walks about like a roaring lion, seeking whom he may devour." (1 Peter 5:8)*

Every garden was a Temple, and every Temple was a house for God. We see this in God's Garden, in Eden's Garden, in the Old Testament Temples, and in the Church's spiritual Temple.

> *"Who serve the copy and shadow of the Heavenly things, as Moses was divinely instructed when he was about to make*

the tabernacle. For he said, 'See that you make all things according to the pattern shown you on the mountain'." (Hebrews 8:5)

"The Lord God planted a garden eastward in Eden, and there He put the man whom He formed." (Genesis 2:8)

"You shall be like a well-watered garden, and like a spring of water, whose waters do not fail." (Isaiah 58:11)

"In whom the whole building, being fitted together, grows into a holy temple in the Lord, in whom you also are being built together for a dwelling place of God in the Spirit." (Ephesians 2:21-22)

"Do you not know that you are the temple of God and that the Spirit of God dwells in you?" (1 Corinthians 3:16)

The stones were in all gardens and temples to remind us "who" we came out of (God), and of our value, worth, and reflection.

"You were the anointed cherub who covers, I established you. You were on the holy mountain of God, you walked back and forth in the midst of fiery stones." (Ezekiel 28:14)

"Now a river went out of Eden... And the gold of that land is good. Bdellium and the onyx stone are there." (Genesis 2:10,12)

"For the Lord will comfort Zion, He will comfort all her waste places, He will make her wilderness like Eden, and her desert like the garden of the Lord." (Isaiah 51:3)

"Now the manna was like coriander seed, and its colour like the colour of bdellium stone." (Numbers 11:7)

"Now for the house of my God I have prepared with all my might: gold for things to be made of gold, silver for the things of silver, bronze for things of bronze, iron for things of iron, wood for things of wood, onyx stones, and stones to be set, glistening stones of various colours, all kinds of precious stones, and marble slabs in abundance."
(1 Chronicles 29:2)

"Coming to Him as to a living stone rejected indeed by men, but chosen by God and precious, you also, as living stones, are being built up a spiritual house, a holy priesthood, to offer up spiritual sacrifices acceptable to God through Jesus Christ."
(1 Peter 2:4-5)

These stones are a revelation to remind us of our "image" –

"For since the creation of the world His invisible attributes are clearly seen, being understood by the things that are made, even His eternal power and Godhead, so that they are without excuse." (Romans 1:20)

Our human body is a Temple and houses a Jewel (our spirit), and when we come into God's glory, gold can manifest from out of our pores, just like the physical Temples were covered with gold. Scripture speaks of our bodies as golden bowls.

"Remember Him, before the silver cord is broken, and the golden bowl is crushed, the pitcher by the wall is shattered, and the wheel at the cistern is crushed; then the dust will return to the earth as it was, and the spirit will return to God who gave it." (Ecclesiastes 12:6-7)

Silver not only speaks of our spirit, but silver was also used as mortar to cement the stones of the physical Temple together.

Then the whole house (Temple) was overlaid with gold and garnished with precious stones for beauty.

> *"The larger room he panelled with cypress which he overlaid with fine gold, and he carved palm trees and chain work on it. And he decorated the house with precious stones for beauty, and the gold was gold from Parvaim."*
> *(2 Chronicles 3:6-7)*

As the pillars in the Temples were covered with gold, gold can manifest on us as we become pillars in the Temple.

> *"You shall hang it upon the four pillars of acacia wood overlaid with gold. Their hooks shall be gold, upon four sockets of silver." (Exodus 26:32)*

> *"And when James, Cephus, and John who seemed to be pillars..." (Galatians 2:9)*

> *"He who overcomes, I will make him a pillar in the temple of My God..." (Revelation 3:12)*

As the physical Temples were decked with precious stones, so does God deck His bride, His people with precious stones in their hands or around them. He adorns them!

> *"For He has clothed me with the garments of salvation, He has covered me with the robe of righteousness. As a Bridegroom decks himself with ornaments, and as a bride adorns herself with jewels. For the earth brings forth its bud, as the garden causes the things that are sown in it to spring forth." (Isaiah 61:10)*

> *"O generation, see the word of the Lord. Have I been a wilderness to Israel or a land of darkness? Why do My people say, We are lords, We will come no more to You?*

Can a virgin forget her ornaments or a bride her attire? Yet My people have forgotten Me days without number." (Jeremiah 2:31-32)

"I will give you the treasures of darkness. And hidden riches of secret places, that you may know that I, the Lord, who call you by name, I Am the God of Israel." (Isaiah 45:3)

"And I will give him a white stone, and on the stone, a new name written which no one knows except him who receives it." (Revelation 2:17)

As the Heavenly Temple is also spoken of as a Bride, as this spiritual Temple overshadows us, this being when the kingdom of Heaven breaks into our realm, manifesting the atmosphere of Heaven, precious stones can and will manifest.

"Then I John, saw the holy city, New Jerusalem, coming down from Heaven from God, prepared as a bride adorned for her husband. And I heard a loud voice from Heaven saying, behold, the tabernacle of God is with men, and He will dwell with them, and they shall be His people. God, Himself will be with them and be their God." (Revelation 21:2-3)

As the Bride of Christ, we are also Holy Priests. And as the Priests of old had precious stones adorned on them, we should expect them to be in our lives too.

"And these are the garments which they shall make, an ephod, a robe, a skilfully woven tunic, a turban, and a sash. So, they shall make holy garments for Aaron, your brother and his sons, that he may minister to Me as priest." (Exodus 28:4)

"You shall make the breastplate of judgement...And you shall put settings of stones in it, four rows of stones. The first row shall be a sardius, a topaz, and an emerald; this shall be the first row, the second row shall be a turquoise, a sapphire, and a diamond, the third row, a jacinth, an agate, and an amethyst, and the fourth row, a beryl, an onyx, and a jasper. They shall be set in gold settings."
(Exodus 28:15; 17-20)

"And you shall put in the breastplate of judgment the Urim and the Thummim, and they shall be over Aarons' heart when he goes in before the Lord." (Exodus 28:30)

"But you are a chosen generation, a royal priesthood, a holy nation, His own special people, that you may proclaim the praises of Him who called you out of darkness into His marvellous light" (1 Peter 2:9)

We are also Kings in Christ as well as a Bride and a Priest.

"Then David took their king's crown from his head, and found it to weigh a talent of gold, and there were precious stones in it. And it was set on David's head."
(1 Chronicles 20:2)

"The king made a great throne of ivory..." and "was covered with precious stones and jewels." (1 Kings 10:18)

"To Him who loved us and washed us from our sins in His own blood, and has made us kings and priests to His God and Father, to Him be glory and dominion forever and ever. Amen." (Revelation 1:5,6)

"For You [Jesus] were slain, and have redeemed us to God by Your blood out of every tribe and tongue and people and nation, and have made us kings and priests to our God; and we shall reign on the earth." (Revelation 5:9b,10)

As we were placed in Christ's breastplate (heart) before the foundation of the world as a hidden treasure, so too, were stones hidden in the breastplate of the Priest, which he wore over his heart. We are in Him, and He is in us. These two stones, the "Urim" and the "Thummim" were used for divine revelation.

> *"In Christ Jesus is hidden all the treasures of wisdom and knowledge" (Colossians 2:3)*

Inside the breastplate, there was a little pocket called 'chosen' where Urim and Thummim were placed. The Urim (Lights) and Thummim (Perfection) hidden in the ephod of the high priest bearing the twelve precious stones of the tribes of Israel represent Jesus Christ hidden within the lineage of the Israelites. Jesus the Urim (Lights) and Thummim (Perfection); within Him, is hidden the wisdom of God and all the children of God.

Scripture says that physical and spiritual stones will cry out, giving revelation.

> *"But He answered and said to them, I tell you that if these should keep silent, the stones would immediately cry out." (Luke 19:40)*

> *"For the stones will cry out from the wall, and the beams from the timbers will echo it." (Habakkuk 2:11)*

> *"You will arise and have mercy on Zion: For the time to favour her, Yes, the set time has come. For your servants take pleasure in her stones, and show favour to her dust." (Psalms 102:13-14)*

> *"Go through the gates! Prepare the way for the people, build up, build up the highway. Take out the stones; lift up a banner for the peoples." (Isaiah 62:10)*

> "Their heart cried out to the Lord, O wall of the daughter of Zion, Let tears run down like a river day and night..." (Lamentations 2:18)

> "And they cried with a loud voice, saying, How Long, O Lord, holy and true, until you judge and avenge our blood on those who dwell on the earth." (Revelation 6:10)

Because our spirit is a Jewel, our spiritual works will be judged according to different "glories" of precious metals and precious stones.

> "Now if anyone builds on this foundation with gold, silver, precious stones, wood, hay or straw, each one's work will become clear, for the day will declare it, because it will be revealed by fire, and the fire will test each one's work, of what sort it is. If anyone's work which he has built on ensures, he will receive a reward. If anyone's work is burned, he will suffer loss, but himself will be saved, yet so as through fire." (1 Corinthians 3:12-15) 62.

> "Look to yourselves, that we do not lose those things we have worked for, but that we may receive a full reward." (2 John 1:8)

It was believed that above the holy of holies, was located the treasury of the kingdom. The word 'treasuries' means 'wealth stored up.' Polished and Glorified spirits are Jewels that will live in the presence of God.

> "For they shall be like the jewels of a crown, lifted like a banner over His land." (Zechariah 9:16)

> *"They shall be mine, says the Lord of hosts, On the day that I make them My jewels, And I will spare them, as a man spares his own son who serves him." (Malachi 3:17)*

> *"But lay up for yourselves treasures in Heaven, where neither moth nor rust destroys and where thieves do not break in and steal. For where your treasure is, there your heart will be also." (Matthew 6:20-21)*

> *"Not that I seek the gift, but I seek the fruit that abounds to your account." (Philippians 4:17)*

There are also two women, describing two kingdoms in the Bible. There is the Bride of Christ, and there is Mystery Babylon the great, the Mother of Harlots. Both these kingdoms are adorned with precious stones, with good and evil intentions. The Bride's stones represent spiritual transformations of God's perfect Image, while the Harlot's stones are physical stones for the lust of wealth on earth.

> *"Then I John, saw the holy city, New Jerusalem coming down out of Heaven from God, prepared as a bride adorned for her husband." (Revelation 21:2)*

> *"The woman was arrayed in purple and scarlet, and adorned with gold and precious stones and pearls, having in her hand a golden cup full of abominations and filthiness of her fornication. And on her forehead a name was written, Mystery Babylon the Great, the Mother of Harlots and of the Abominations of the earth." (Revelation 17:4-5)*

We must be clear that the Mother of Harlot's stones are earthly precious stones for wealth. We cannot judge and just say the stones, that are manifesting in churches around the world today, are from the devil. Her stones are said to be used for trading on the earth.

> *"The kings of the earth who committed fornication and lived luxuriously with her will weep and lament for her, when they see the smoke of her burning." (Revelation 18:9)*

> *"And the merchants of the earth will weep and mourn over her, for no one buys their merchandise anymore." (Revelation 18:11)*

> *"Merchandise of gold and silver, precious stones and pearls, fine linen and purple, silk and scarlet, every kind of citron wood, every kind of object of ivory, every kind of object of most precious wood, iron, and marble..." (Revelation 18:12)*

The precious stones of the Bride of Christ will always carry a pure, beautiful 'mystery' for they have, throughout time on earth and in Heaven. The precious stones are the mystery of the Church, being in Christ from the foundation of the world. They speak and reveal to those who have eyes to see and blind those who are not His. For the mystery of ages is that God's grace would perfect, and polish stones that carry and shine the fullness of Him, His people, His Bride.

> *"However, we speak wisdom among those who are mature, yet not the wisdom of this age, nor of the rulers of this age, who are coming to nothing. But we speak the wisdom of God in a mystery, the hidden wisdom which God ordained before the ages for our glory, which none of the rulers of this age knew, for had they known, they would not have crucified the Lord of glory." (1 Corinthians 2:6-7)*

> *"This is the great mystery, but I speak concerning Christ and the Church." (Ephesians 5:32)*

The Bride of Christ is spoken of as a city, and Believers are individual living stones in the spiritual city. And all our

precious stones and memorial stones will shine in the walls of salvation around us in the spiritual Temple, reflecting the full spectrum of God's fullness in glorious colours.

> "We have a strong city; God will appoint salvation for walls and bulwarks. Open the gates that the righteous nation, which keeps the truth, may enter in."
> (Isaiah 26:1-2)
>
> "But you shall call your walls Salvation and your gates Praise." (Isaiah 60:18)
>
> "Behold I will lay your stones with colourful gems. And lay your foundations with sapphires. I will make your pinnacles of rubies, your gates of crystal. And all your walls of precious stones." (Isaiah 54:11- 12)
>
> "The construction of its wall was jasper, and the city was pure gold, like clear glass. The foundations of the wall of the city were adorned with all kinds of precious stones, the first foundation was jasper, the second sapphire, the third chalcedony, the fourth emerald, the fifth sardonyx, the sixth sardius, the seventh chrysolite, the eighth beryl, the ninth topaz, the tenth chrysoprase, the eleventh jacinth, and the twelfth amethyst. The twelve gates were twelve pearls each individual gate was one pearl. And the street of the city was pure gold, like transparent glass." (Revelation 21: 18-21)

The day will come when Jesus will return and bring Heaven to earth. The Temple of God will come down and manifest on earth and expel all wickedness.

> "Now I saw a new Heaven and a new earth, for the first Heaven and the first earth had passed away (restored). Also, there was no more sea. Then I, John saw the holy city, New Jerusalem coming down out of Heaven from God, prepared as a bride adorned for her husband. And I heard

a loud voice from Heaven saying, behold, the tabernacle of God is with men, and he will dwell with them, and they shall be His people. God himself will be with them and be their God" (Revelation 21:1-3)

"And he carried me away in the Spirit to a great mountain, and showed me the great city, the holy Jerusalem, descending out of Heaven from God, having the glory of God. Her light was like a most precious stone, like a jasper stone, clear as crystal."
(Revelation 21:10-11)

"But the cowardly, unbelieving, abominable, murderers, sexually immoral, sorcerers, idolaters, and all liars shall have their part in the lake which burns with fire and brimstone, which is the second death." (Revelation 21:8)

Bibliography

Alec, W. (2005), *The Fall of Lucifer*. Warboys Publishing Ltd
Alec, W. (2013) *Visions of Heaven*. Warboys Publishing Ltd
Alport, O. (February 2019). *Was There Enough – or too much?* Retrieved June 2019, from https://hamodia.com/columns/was-there-enough-or-too-much/
Arns, M. David (2014), *Gold Dust, Jewels, & More: Manifestations of God*.
Beale, G.K (2004), *The Temple and the Church's Mission*. InterVarsity Press.
Beale, S. Stephen Beale, (Nov 2017), *Why do Christians Get White Stones in Heaven?* Retrieved June 2019 from https://catholicexchange.com/ christians-get-white-stones-heaven
Cauley, M. (2012) *The Outer Darkness*, Misthological Press.
Cauley, M. (2021) *Redeemed Bodies Versus Glorified Bodies*, Misthological Press.
Clayton, I. (2016), *Realms of the Kingdom, Volume Two*. Sons of Thunder Publications.
Clayton, I. (2014), *Realms of the Kingdom, Volume One,* Seraph Creative Publishers.
Crowder, J. (2009), *The Ecstasy of Loving God*. Destiny Image Publishers.
Cruz, L (2007), *All His Jewels: From Glory to Glory*. Xulon Press.
Curtis, A. (2019), *Talk With Me in Paradise*. Kin & Kingdom Books.
Curtis, A. (2023), *Explore With Me In Paradise, Book Two,* Kin & Kingdom Books.
Dye, D. (2016), *The Temple in Creation: A Portrait of the Family*. Foundations in Torah Publishing.
Dye, D. (2015), *The Temple in The Garden: Priests and Kings*. Foundations in Torah Publishing.
Edwards, J. (2005) *Charity and Its Fruit*. The Banner of Truth Trust.

Enklin, A. (2015 January), *Living Torah: Leaving Egypt and Looking to the Future*. Retrieved June 25, 2019 from http://Unitedwithisrael.org/living-torah-leaving-egypt-and- looking-to-the-future/

Fellows, R. (2019), *Wilderness Like Eden*, Self-Published.

Fellows, R. (2019), *Granny Rainbow Shekinah*, Self-Published.

Fellows, R. (2021), *Heaven Through the Eyes of Children*, Self-Published.

Fellows, R. (2022), *The Fathers Garden*, Self-Published.

Fellows, R. (2023), *Pre-existence; The Hidden Mystery*, Self-Published.

Gallups, C. (2018), *Gods of Ground Zero, The Truth of Eden's Iniquity*. Defender Publishing

Hardinge, L. (2011) *Stones OF Fire*. American Christian Ministries.

Healy, B. K. (2018), *The Veil: An Invitation to the Unseen Realm*, Charisma House.

Heiser, S. M. (2015), *The Unseen Realm: Recovering the supernatural worldview of the Bible*, Lexham Press. Ilani, Z. *Diamonds and Gemstones in Judaica*. Published by Harry Oppenheimer Diamond Museum.

Heflin, R. (2000), *Golden Glory; The New Wave of Signs and Wonders*, McDougal Publishing.

Lisorkin Eyzenberg, E., Retrieved June 2019, from https://israelbiblicalstudies.com/bible-jewish-studies/#bible-studies

King, C. M. (2016), *Gemstones from Heaven*, Self-Published.

Maloney, J. (2011), *Ladies of Gold: The Remarkable Ministry Of The Golden Candlestick*. West-Bow Press.

Missler, Chuck (2000), Chuck Missler, *Hidden Treasures in the Biblical Text*. Koinonia House.

Mouliert, G. (2011), *The Breastplate of the High Priest: Unlocking the Mystery of the Living Stones*. Keeper Publishing.

Neusner, J. (2001), *A Theological Commentary to the Midrash: Song of Song Rabbat*.

Pease, G. (2014), *The Jewels of Heaven*. Retrieved June 2019 from https://sermons.faithlife.com/sermons/124750-the-jewels-of-heaven

Pitre, B. (2014), *Jesus the Bridegroom: The Greatest Love Story Ever Told*. Crown Publishing.

Prempeh-Dapaah, A. (2018) *Laying Up Treasures in Heaven*, Stonewall Press.

Price, Paula A., PhD. (2004), *Before the Garden: God's Eternal Continuum*. Flaming Vision Publications.

Price, R. (1997), *The Stones cry Out*. World of Bible Ministries Inc

Rosenfeld, D. (n.d.) *Urim and Thummim*. Retrieved June 2019 from https://www.aish.com/atr/Urim-and-Thummim.html.

Schwartz, Howard. (2004), *Tree of Souls, The Mythology of Judaism*, Oxford University Press Publishers.

Scott, E. (2010), *40 Days in Heaven; The True Testimony of Seneca Sodi's Visitation to Paradise, the Holy City and the Glory of God's Throne,* First Fruit Offering Publishers.

Smith, G. & T. (2014), *Gemstones from Heaven*. Netturtle Studios Publishing.

Stone, P. (2015), *Chronicles of the Sacred Mountain*. Voice of Evangelism Outreach Ministries.

Storms, S. (n.d.), *The Letter to The Church at Pergamum (2:12-17)*. Retrieved June 2019 from https://www.samstorms.com/all-articles/post/the-letter-to-the-church-at-pergamum--2:12-17-

Trask, M. (2009), *The 12 Gemstones of Revelation: Unlocking the Significance of the Gemstones Phenomenon*. Destiny Image Publishers.

OTHER BOOKS BY RICHARD FELLOWS

All books are available at online bookstores worldwide, or direct from author – richfellows@hotmail.com

Wilderness Like Eden, **Published 2019. ISBN 978-0-648-58830-6**

The supernatural appearing of gemstones from Heaven, around the world, is on the increase as faithful Christians worship God and cry out for the joining of Heaven and earth. What is this phenomenon? How is it related to the God of the Bible?

In *Wilderness Like Eden*, these questions are addressed in the light of God's Heavenly Kingdom intimately clothing Eden, the Bride and the Sons of God – their functions and callings in the earth.

Richard lays out the Biblical Theology from Genesis to Revelation, bringing an understanding to the gemstone phenomenon.

Granny Rainbow Shekinah, **Published 2019. ISBN 978-0-648-58832-0**

Throughout history, God has revealed Himself in His creation. In The Garden of Eden, he visited earth in Theophanies in the Old Testament, in the incarnation of Jesus, and also in disguise, after His resurrection and ascension into Heaven. But what of the Holy Spirit, what is His image and likeness? What is the Holy Spirit's "form" and essence as the Spirit of Glory? In Granny Rainbow Shekinah, these questions and more are addressed. Come on a journey as we go behind the veil!

Heaven Through the Eyes of Children, **Published 2021.**
ISBN 978-0-648-58834-4

When a Theologian encounters Heaven himself, his heart is opened to believe like a child, and is challenged by a small community of children in the jungles of India, experiencing visions of Heaven. Hidden in the remote mountain, a remarkable outpouring of the Holy Spirit touched a community and revealed the reality of Jesus and His Kingdom in Heaven.

This is a Theologian's journey of analysing the geographical landscape of Heaven based on their testimonies. From the eyes of children, through the mind of a Theologian, the truth is revealed.

The Father's Garden, **Published 2022.   ISBN 978-0-648-58835-1**

Following on from his previous book, Heaven through the eyes of Children, Richard Fellows now brings us to a more detailed description of a specific area of Heaven – the Father's Garden.

Based on various accounts of people throughout the ages, we are given insight into areas of Heaven not often explored before. Few people have the privilege of actually going into these areas and being able to come back to our realm and describe them, but more recently, these areas have been made known to us, to encourage us to look forward to the day we will see Father God face to face. Step inside, and journey through the Father's Garden with Richard!

Pre-Existance – The Hidden Mystery, **Published 2023.**
ISBN 978-0-648-58836-8

What is Man that God is mindful of him? An ape, a man of dust from the earth, or a Mystery? What is this Mystery that was hidden in God's wisdom before the ages (1 Cor. 2:7), before the foundation of the world, to be holy and without blame kept secret in the Garden chamber, the fortress under the shadow of the Almighty? Come on a deep journey to reveal the Mystery of "who" we really are, 'in the beauties of holiness, from the womb of the dawn' (Psalm 110:3). 'For in Him, we live, move and have our being' (Acts 17:28). Let our eyes be opened – 'For many see dimly in a mirror' (1 Cor. 13:12).

In this book, the author lays out an extensive Biblical theology, drawing on many verses, combined with revelation, ancient texts, early church fathers' interpretations, Biblical scholarship and early Jewish literature in revealing the Mystery. Written in the spirit of an apologetic defence, one step at a time.

www.ingramcontent.com/pod-product-compliance
Lightning Source LLC
Chambersburg PA
CBHW031249290426
44109CB00012B/506